# JOURNEYS FROM HERE TO ETERNITY

*by*
DR. CURTIS ALEXANDER

JOURNEYS FROM HERE TO ETERNITY

Copyright © 2024 by Curtis E. Alexander

Visit www.leadershipbooks.net
Address requests for information to:
Leadership Books, Inc.
1489 West Warm Springs Road, Suite 110
Henderson, NV 89014
Support@leadershipbooks.net

Library of Congress Cataloging–in–Publication data
Hardcover: 978-1-951648-95-4
Paperback: 978-1-951648-96-1
eBook: 978-1-951648-97-8

Alexander, Curtis, 1952–
JOURNEYS FROM HERE TO ETERNITY / Curtis Alexander

Unless otherwise noted, all Scripture readings are from The Holy Bible, New International Version® NIV®. Copyright © 1973, 1978, 1984, 2011 by Biblica Inc.® Used by permission of Biblica, Inc.® All rights reserved worldwide.

New American Standard Bible® NASB® Copyright © 1960, 1971, 1977, 1995, 2020 by The Lockman Foundation A Corporation Not for Profit La Habra, CA All Rights Reserved www.lockman.org

Holy Bible, New Living Translation, copyright © 1996, 2004, 2015 by Tyndale House Foundation. All Rights Reserved. Used by permission of Tyndale House Publishers, Carol Stream, Illinois 60188. All rights reserved.

Any internet addresses, websites, blogs, etc., in this book are offered as a resource. They are not intended in any way to be or imply an endorsement by Leadership Books, Incorporated, nor does LBI vouch for the content of these resources for the life of this book.

All rights reserved. No part of this publication may be reproduced, stored in a retrieval system, or transmitted in any form or by any means—electronic, mechanical, photocopy, re-cording or any other—except for brief quotations, without the prior permission of the publisher.

Printed in the United States of America

# *Dedication*

This book is dedicated to my Mother, Anna Batterbee Alexander. She aspired to be an author, and published several projects. Alas, she had so many interests, she never reached the heights of any.

By the time I became Associate Editor of a national denominational magazine (2003), she was gone to heaven. But I said then, "Mom would be so pleased." When I earned my Doctorate I reiterated that sentiment. I said it again, later, when I was selected as Academic Dean of Covenant Bible Seminary. And I repeated myself one more time when Michael Stickler, Publisher of Leadership Books, Inc., sent me contracts for BEING LIKE JESUS: 100 Days to More Success, Satisfaction and Living on Purpose; and for this book, JOURNEYS FROM HERE TO ETERNITY.

My Father was a Pastor for three decades, and I heard hundreds of his sermons. Yet, I find myself quoting Mom most often. She was a godly, compassionate, industrious woman of Proverbs 31. She's been gone twenty-nine years, but in so many ways, is still influencing me and my family to live for Jesus.

# *Acknowledgment*

*Any author is but one member of a publishing team. It takes contributions from many to complete an involved project like this.*

*The Leadership Books team, led by Michael Stickler (publisher), Faith Burns (longsuffering Managing Editor), and the design and promotion staffs have incorporated the efforts of many to make this book a reality.*

*I also acknowledge the many, many parishioners who, over the years, have given me more than I was ever able to give them. Here's a warmhearted thank you to all those good people in Battle Creek, MI, Van Wert, OH, Gaylord, MI, Mancelona, MI, Petoskey, MI, Groveland, IL, Bliss, MI, Roy, WA, and Elma WA. You—and God—helped me become the servant I am today.*

# *Endorsements*

"As you let this book guide your walk with Jesus, triumph in Christ will increasingly become yours. I recommend this book, as it will lead to freedom and fullness in Christ."

— REV. DR. TOM MURPHY, *former Editor–in–Chief, Missionary Church Today magazine.*

"I can feel faith rising up in me as I read."

— HEATHER COMSTOCK, *founder of Arcadian Hill Handmade.*

Reader beware: your life could be changed by reading this book. My friend and former mentor, Curtis Alexander, has sounded the clarion call that our relationship with God is not about destination, but journey. For some, he has resurrected this powerful metaphor, reminding us that our life is a walk with Christ. For others, this idea of journeying with God is an entirely new and life altering concept.

— REV. MICHAEL MCGLYNN, BATTLE CREEK, MICHIGAN

In Journeys From Here to Eternity, Dr. Alexander bids you ride with him through Bible times all the way to the present. As a truck driver, turned lawyer, turned judge, I couldn't resist jamming a few gears with Dr. A. My journey took me through family ties, mountaintop and valley experiences, and being humbled. Yours may run through witnessing opportunities, hurdling obstacles, or choosing which stand to take. Whatever your journey, Pastor Curt has the map.

— JUDGE MICHAEL RISINGER (RET.), ILLINOIS AND FLORIDA

It was encouraging and intriguing to read Journeys From Here to Eternity. I found the writing informative, concise, and the lessons applicable. Moments of truth were included in each chapter, and appeared all through the writing. It is an engaging and enjoyable read.

— REV. DENNY COLLINS, MICHIGAN

This is a "Must-Read" for all believers in Jesus wondering where they're headed in life. As Dr. Alexander teaches, "Long ago God mapped the route you are traveling on today." He wants to lead you on a journey through suffering, depression, and danger to peace, forgiveness, and friendship. You can serve and fulfill God's plan for your life. Curtis uses stories, lesson summaries, breakout boxes, Moment of Truth circles, reflection questions, and YouTube videos—cutting edge formatting—to connect with the reader in every chapter. The lessons are powerful yet easy to read for anyone. Open this book and be pulled into blessing and intrigue. You can't put it down!

— JERRY BREWER, FLORIDA

Curtis, I enjoyed and appreciate your God–gifted wisdom and skills in writing such a refreshing, insightful and challenging book! May it be a blessing to all who get hold of it!

Remembering the past always gives opportunity to live more wisely and blessed in the present. Curtis Alexander's Journeys From Here to Eternity refreshingly invites us to adhere to our Way Maker's unshakeable faithfulness and be challenged to have Him map our personal life's journey. I encourage you to join him in this adventure!

— REV. JERRY TERUI, KAUAI, HAWAII

Curtis uses simple language and inspiring stories to apply deep biblical truth from familiar Bible women and men. He redraws stories we think we know, with a twist—their journey. We focus on the obvious, but these stories are more than a Sunday School lesson. Each journey is different and key to who the person was, and why God used them. If we are willing, their journeys can help us on ours, and shape us into who God wants us to be. Discover the journeys of these characters, and in the process learn about your own.

— REV. MICHAEL ALEXANDER, MICHIGAN *(Dr. A's nephew)*

*JOURNEYS From Here to Eternity* explores several dynamic Bible stories (and their characters) who encounter risk, reward, and eventually, renewal. Author Dr. Curtis Alexander uses his decades of research, teaching and communicating to bring fresh perspective on how we can find joy and purpose throughout our own life's journey. The book culminates with the life of Jesus Christ, and ultimately encourages believers that: *"A passion for biblical wisdom and insight demands a lifetime journey. It will be worth every expense, every hardship, every demand."* This is a must-read for Christians living in times of uncertainty, and one that I believe will stand the test of time.

— JOSEPH BAKER, TEXAS

# TABLE OF CONTENTS

Perpetual Motion, an Introduction .................................................... xi
Destination Unknown: *Abraham* ........................................................ 1
Over Hill, Over Dale, We Will Hit the Dusty Trail: *Joseph* ................. 9
Love's Long Journey: *Ruth and Naomi* .............................................. 19
There's Bad News and There's Good News: *Philip* ............................ 31
Roadmap to Peace: *Abigail* ............................................................... 41
No Pain, No Gain: *Job* ...................................................................... 51
A Mother's Worst Nightmare: *Mary, mother of Jesus* ....................... 63
Slip Out the Back, Jack: *Elijah* .......................................................... 75
Walk on the Wild Side: *Esther* .......................................................... 85
Like a Good Neighbor: *The Good Samaritan* .................................... 93
A Bowl of Rocky Road: *Nehemiah* ................................................. 101
A Tale of Two Friendships: *The Shunammite Woman* .................... 111
Home Where You Belong: *The Prodigal Father* .............................. 119
The Great Detour: *Saul who became Paul* ...................................... 127
Humble Highway: *Naaman* ............................................................ 137
Deal or No Deal: *Hannah* ............................................................... 145
Return to the Scene of the Crime: *Moses* ....................................... 155
The Long and Winding Road: *The Queen of Sheba* ....................... 167
Road to Redemption: *the Daniel Model* ......................................... 177
Women of Courage: *Deborah and Jael* ........................................... 187
Road to Rejection: *Jesus* ................................................................. 199
Been There, Done That: *an Epilogue* ............................................. 205

# PERPETUAL MOTION
## AN INTRODUCTION

Life is a journey—better yet, a never-ending highway of rush-hour, bumper-to-bumper journeys. We turn homeward to heal old wounds, bury our dead, or perhaps rediscover a lost friendship. We revisit our greatest victory and sweat through our most humiliating defeat. We hit the road on a quest for wisdom, to fulfill a dream, right a wrong, or explore the beckoning horizon. We agonize through grief and pain, maybe follow God's path to redeem the evil culture around us.

Life is nothing if not a constant panorama of changing scenery, anxious confrontations, new experiences, joyful celebrations, and great adventures waiting to be joined.

Some of life's journeys produce a pounding pulse and pumping adrenalin. Others are pursued with dread and dragging of feet. Occasionally, we stifle a yawn. Whatever your experiences, **life is a journey of constant movement;** sometimes slow and serene, sometimes a blinding blur. But always, movement.

I once drove an Army eighteen-wheeler, hauling military machinery into the mountains of Hawaii. In creeper gear, we had to watch the tires to be sure we were still mov-

> **Surrender control to God. He'll never lead you wrong!**

ing; progress was that slow. But in the 101st Airborne (Air Assault), the ground beneath the low-flying helicopter would be a dizzying flash, a blinding blur.

Movies, television, and popular culture all contribute to our conception of *JOURNEY:* Back to the Future, On the Road Again, Follow the Yellow Brick Road, Up the Down Staircase, The Long and Winding Road, Cat's in the Cradle, From Here to Eternity, Star Trek: Voyager. They say entertainment mirrors life. And motion is at the heart of Hollywood. Yes, art mirrors life.

Can we agree? **Life *is* perpetual motion.** Crawling by or speeding past, life is always, always moving. Sometimes it's maddeningly slow, and we wish we could hit fast-forward. Other times, we wish we could push 'pause' just to catch our breath. And we wonder how, in the flood of activity, can I have a solid foundation under all the shifting quicksand of today's relativism?

The Bible is full of men and women who might have wondered the same thing. With no internet, eight-lane expressways or airport hubs, they still found life to be one journey after another. And their experiences point the way to bedrock beneath our daily temblors.

*Abraham* set out on Canaan Boulevard, destination unknown. He trusted the Divine Dispatcher to guide his travels.

*Ruth* discarded a mundane, ho-hum life to risk it all across the barren mountains of southern Israel. She risked the journey to take up life in a strange culture, traveling with the adopted mother she had come to love.

*Joseph* was clueless about why his life was so troubled. But he held onto his godly values as his roller coaster ride flung him one way, then another. Finally, he found his calling—Prime Minister of the world's greatest superpower! "Ah, now I get it!"

Jesus's mother *Mary* found herself on a journey that ended in every mother's worst nightmare; except grief was not the end of the story.

*Saul*, a.k.a. *Paul*, walked the Roman pavement of the first century, spreading the Good News of Jesus Christ, until his earthly journey ended just outside Rome's mean walls.

*Moses* had to go home and confront his criminal past before he could save his people and Charlton Heston could play his signature role of a lifetime.

*Abigail* made a short Nobel Peace Prize journey, and found the love of her life.

The *Queen of Sheba* followed the flowing Nile in a lengthy search for truth and wisdom.

*Elijah*'s headlong dash to Sinai was depressing until he heard God's quiet, sane voice of reason. He went on to influence a nation for eternity.

*Esther* tempted fate to save her people from oblivion.

*The Prodigal Father* made a short but madcap dash to welcome home his recalcitrant son. They were whirlwind journeys all, with little chance to catch their breath!

What journey are you on right now? Is it thrilling, terrifying, agonizing, or confusing? Where will your next journey go? **Long ago, God mapped the route you travel today. He charted your path.** He knows every pothole. And He is eager to go with you where your road will lead, even if you have followed rabbit trails along the way. **He is, after all, the God of Plan B.**

Is God your co-pilot? Rather, are you *His* co-pilot? One of humankind's most challenging exercises is to take your hands off the controls and let Him fly.

Enjoy the trip, and journeying mercies to you!

Curtis Alexander, Palmetto, Florida, 2024

# 1
# DESTINATION UNKNOWN

### JOURNEY TO THE INTERSECTION OF 'TRUST' AND 'OBEY'
— Abraham —
(Genesis 11:31; 12:1–13:18; 17:5)

## IT'S AN ADVENTURE

N*shima* is a corn–based porridge and it makes its mother proud—its mother is wallpaper paste! But according to a Zambian friend, though bland and unappetizing, *nshima* has staved off generations of starvation in his African country. The culinary delights of Zambia were not the highlight of my missions trip. But food is always part of the adventure when one travels in the two–thirds world.

I couldn't bring myself to sample the rubbery tentacles of squid in Hong Kong. I never got up the courage to taste those little rubber bands covered with culinary suction cups. Adventure batted her eyes. She flirted. She beckoned. She sang her siren song. But I held out for hot dogs. Years later, I ate Peruvian *paella* and swallowed the tiny squid tentacles—no problem.

When Kathy and I visited our missionary kids in Greece, she had a great attitude about that largely untested, back–street Mediterranean quadrant of the gastronomic galaxy. This shy country girl, who as a youngster could not eat in a restaurant if someone was looking at her, was eager to try all kinds of new things. In her own words, "It's an adventure!"

In Greece, the rest of us ordered safe things like pizza, Greek salad, and baklava, but she ordered mussels in a mysterious brine ("are you sure that's not *turpentine?*"). When they asked if we liked seafood, I pictured Red Lobster®. She said she would try the calamari and got deep-fried octopus. She loved the adventure!

On Crete we saw goats climbing in the trees. In one case, they were hanging out into space, with only a horizontal tree trunk and the Mediterranean Sea below to break their fall. They didn't.

We paid more for a hotel room in Cookstown, Northern Ireland than we sometimes paid for whole vacations. In the dining room they were playing Michael Jackson and Momma Cass! I grumbled to the waitress, "I didn't come six thousand miles to hear this. Don't you have some authentic Irish music?" Imagine a Motown adventure in a quaint Irish village!

We chanced narrow, winding roads (and driving on the left) in Ireland's rural interior to find Avoca, the film site of the BBC drama *Ballykissangel*. Another adventure we'll never forget!

The London double-decker sightseeing bus that was supposed to take us all the way back to our hotel—did not. It stopped at Hyde Park Corner, done for the day! We walked through the heart of Knightsbridge, past world-famous Harrod's Department Store, Prince Albert Hall and The Natural History Museum. Our feet throbbed, but a ruddy good adventure it was, Old Chap!

We rode the underground Tube to All Souls Church, not knowing what to expect. It was the week after the USA seized Baghdad. Would we stand out as *Yankees*? Would we be singled out as non-Anglican? Instead, it was a heartwarming, blessed experience—a wonderful adventure in worship; warm and rewarding!

## SCARY AND SCINTILLATING

**The unknown can indeed be threatening, unsettling, perhaps even scary.** But it can also lead to exhilarating adventures. A friend loaded up his motor home, drove to the end of the driveway, and said to his wife, "Ruthie, do you wanna go left or right?" And that's how their vacation began. An adventure at every turn!

That paints a wonderful picture of life. Every day brings a journey into the unknown. We can fear it, curse it, run from it, even hide in our room with the curtains drawn. Or we can embrace it as a God-given adventure and experience the ride of a lifetime.

Imagine being a wealthy, powerful man with a large staff and extended family that depended on you for everything. You were settled, established, and successful. Oh, by the way, you were seventy-five years old. (And you don't know it yet, but you still have a hundred years to live!) Then God says, "I want you to pack up everything and hit the road. But I'm not telling you where to go just yet. Trust Me and get going!"

So, Abram (who became Abraham) packed up the motor home, drove to the end of the driveway, and said, "Sarah, should we go left or right?" So began a great adventure that resulted in God's blessing upon the whole human race through all of history to follow (Genesis 12:1–5; Hebrews 11:8–16).

## BLIND RECKONING

**Make a journey away from evil.** Abraham's old stomping ground was idol-infested Ur of the Chaldees, a bastion of pagan wickedness. God wanted to plant His chosen people in a place free from Ur's idolatrous evil, so He sent Abraham on a magnificent journey. Not that God always moves His people away from evil places. Sometimes He sends them *to* a pagan place, like Jonah to Nineveh, to influence it for Christ. But for the patriarch of His chosen people, God wanted a clean break, a fresh start, a new beginning, a "destination unknown."

God called Abraham to put feet to his faith. He was wealthy and owned lots of stuff. Many servants and family members depended on him. So, moving was more than just a hassle; it was a radical rearrangement of life. Abraham came through because he trusted God. Because of his faith, he obeyed, left his home and went out by blind reckoning. "He trusted God, so he obeyed!" is a recurring theme in Abraham's epic story: son of longtime Chaldean Terah, world traveler, servant of God, patriarch, man of trust and obedience, ancestor of the world's Savior!

**Faith and obedience are committed partners for life.** People can obey without trusting, but usually only if force is threatened or applied. Call it obedience under duress—not God's way. If we trust God, then we'll feel safe to obey Him. Even if God gives commands that seem contradictory or unreasonable, our trust in Him will result in willing, faithful obedience.

> **Trust and obey, for there's no other way to be happy in Jesus, but to trust and obey.**

Because trust and obedience were partners in Abraham's long, fruitful life, we know him as a giant of the Faith. And just think of the outlandish things God asked of Abraham.

"Leave your home and go to a place I'm not revealing to you right now."

"Trust me to give you a son, even though you're ninety years old and Sarah, your wife, is eighty. By the way, it won't happen for another ten years!"

"Take your special, one-of-a-kind son, Isaac, to Mt. Moriah and sacrifice him there as a burnt offering to Me. Yeah, I know, I said no human sacrifices. Just trust and obey Me on this!"

God never explained Himself at the time. Only later would He make things clear to Abraham. But the patriarch trusted, so he obeyed even when the destination was vague. He made one journey after another, acceding to God's "unreasonable" demands, always trusting, always obeying. His trust led to obedience, and as a result, his obedience led to God's rich and vibrant blessings. Abraham discovered that God was always faithful and always worthy of trust. "Trust and obey" is the heavenly adventure!

Join the dynamic duo. Superficial trust in the Lord isn't sufficient to move us to active obedience. Yet God calls us to make the connection between real, deep–down trust and practical obedience that might lead us to head for parts unknown—if not actually to sacrifice our firstborn! When we join the dynamic duo of trust and obedience, we can hold on and enjoy the ride, even when we don't know where the journey will lead. And who of us ever knows just where life's journey will end up?

Trust partnered with obedience delivers the pinnacle of adventure. Webster defines *adventure* as "an exciting or very unusual experience; participation in exciting undertakings or enterprises."

## BTW

- **Abraham** could have had the "Poor Me!" syndrome: no heir; stuck in limbo for years; wife troubles with lecherous kings; nephew took the fertile land and left him with dry ground; wells filled in.

- God told Abraham to offer his son Isaac as a burnt offering. It was the ultimate sacrifice after waiting 100 years for this son!

- But God produced miracle after miracle to bless Abraham and his family. A childless patriarch (there's a misnomer), the barren couple became parents to a nation and blessed 4,000 years of human history.

- God can be trusted, even if you can't figure out what He's doing. God is totally trustworthy.

- **THE LESSON:** Never underestimate God and His miracle–working power. He loves you richly and His timing is perfect—more than you know. When you can't trace His plan for you, trust His loving, faithful heart.

God has wonderful things in mind for His followers. If you trust enough to obey, you'll begin to experience the exciting adventure God intends your life to be. Let it be said, what's wonderful to one of us might not be so wonderful to someone else. My educational odyssey doesn't appeal to many. To me, it's been a wonderful adventure...attending sixteen different schools from kindergarten (in a one-room rural school) through doctoral degree.

A friend spent his life growing corn, soybeans, and hogs on the Prairies of Illinois—not most people's idea of adventure. But his life also included travel to more than a hundred different destinations around the world, including a frostbite-inducing, toe-numbing adventure to the North Pole! Many would not find all that travel enticing. They'd rather curl up by the fireplace at home than see the world. Their idea of adventure is domesticated.

A woman I know willingly rode a bus hundreds of miles with dozens of other women just to go shopping. To her it was a great adventure. To some of us an IRS audit is preferred!

Another parishioner, a nurse just a few years from retirement, moved to South Africa, where she ministered to desperately ill people. She was thrilled almost beyond words by the prospect of using her medical skills and training to assist the Great Physician in an African nation ravaged by HIV/AIDS. For her, there was no greater adventure in the world than medical ministry in remote Tugela Ferry. Most of us might agree with Scott Wesley Brown's plaintive-but-amusing prayer, "Please don't send me to Africa!"[1] But there are others, thank God, for whom such a life journey is a wonderful, not-to-be-missed adventure. When trust in God partners with obedience, God blesses in fabulous, unexpected ways. Let the adventure begin!

**We all have different tastes.** A great adventure to one is terrifying, boring, or just plain weird to another. God wants to meet each of us

---

[1] YouTube: Please Don't Send Me to Africa – Scott Wesley Brown

where we are, and journey with us to the most wonderful places we can imagine. It may be "destination unknown" to you now, but the adventure—and the blessing—is waiting. For anyone who trusts God enough to obey even when the roadmap seems blank or blurry, God has exciting plans—the adventure of a lifetime.

That's what Abraham's story is all about: **trust God to lead you to the best place He most wants you to be**, and revel in the excitement! In fact, the journey itself is pure adventure. If you trust God enough to obey Him, He will bless your life with exciting journeys, wonderful places and fascinating opportunities. The Lord knows your destination. Faithful trust and obedience will change the entire trajectory of your life!

---

### MOMENT OF TRUTH
God makes heartwarming promises to those
who trust and obey Him, to those who honor their promises
to Him and fulfill their duties to Christ.

---

**MY PERSONAL JOURNEY:** God once tried to send me on a journey, but I wouldn't go. It happened like this:

_____
_____
_____
_____
_____

- I would describe my fears and hesitancy to go as:

_____
_____
_____

_____

_____

_____

- I trust God enough that I will obey, even if I don't know where the journey will lead, or what it will require. ❏ Yes   ❏ No

- Here's a description of the adventure God may be sending me on:
_____

_____

_____

_____

_____

# 2

# OVER HILL, OVER DALE, WE WILL HIT THE DUSTY TRAIL

**JOURNEY FROM VALLEY TO MOUNTAINTOP**
— Joseph —
(Genesis 37–50)

## LIFE'S UPS AND DOWNS

Everyone I know agrees that life has its ups and downs. Even the best life seldom goes the way we would script it. For some, life's "downs" are deep indeed. If you need convincing, consider the following accident claim supposedly filed with a health insurance company.

I'm an amateur radio operator. I was working alone at the top of my new eighty-foot ham radio tower. When I finished I discovered I had brought up about three hundred pounds of tools and spare hardware. Rather than carry the now unneeded tools and material down by hand, I decided to lower the items in a barrel. Fortunately, a pulley was still attached to the tower. I went to the top and loaded everything into the barrel. Then I went back to the ground and untied the rope, holding it tightly to ensure a slow descent of the 300 pounds of tools (BTW, I weigh only one-hundred-fifty-five pounds).

**Surprised at being jerked off the ground so suddenly, I held onto the rope.** Naturally, I proceeded at speed up the tower. About halfway up, I met the barrel coming down. This explains my concussion and broken collarbone (see claims form). Slowed only slightly, I continued my rapid ascent, not stopping until my fingers were three knuckles deep in the pulley.

Fortunately, I had regained my presence of mind and held onto the rope despite my pain. Unfortunately, the barrel of tools hit the ground and the bottom broke out. Emptied of tools, the barrel now weighed about forty pounds. Remember, I weigh 155 pounds.

Predictably, I began a rapid descent down the side of the tower. At about the forty-foot level, I met the barrel coming back up. This explains my fractured ankles and lacerations to my legs and lower body. Hitting the barrel slowed me and minimized my injuries when I fell onto the pile of tools. Thankfully, only three vertebrae were cracked. As I lay there on the tools, writhing in pain, unable to stand and eying the empty barrel eighty feet above me, I again lost my focus. I let go of the rope and the barrel landed on my head—hence, the skull fracture (X-rays to come).

So what if www.snopes.com claimed this story is more fiction than fact? The fact is, "We're all well aware of 'Life's Ups and Downs!'"

The biblical story of Joseph, he of the Technicolor® dream coat, tells of a life full of extreme highs and lows. His approach to an up-and-down life and his vision of the big picture are wonderful lessons, learned in the pounding surf of life's turbulent seas. Here's the itinerary for us all.

## JOSEPH'S JOURNEY

**The journey leads through valleys and mountaintops galore.** Joseph started life high in the foothills. Not king of the mountain, but surely a chosen prince on the ascending slopes. Favorite son of his wealthy father Jacob, he was born to his father's favorite wife Rachel. And his first seventeen years were mostly idyllic. The only problem he encountered was an immature ego trip and the resulting conflict with his brothers because of his status. We could call Joseph's start *'Mountaintop Number One.'*

About this time, his jealous brothers threw him into an empty well, then sold him into slavery (a drastic measure just to curb his youthful ego). Welcome to *'Valley Number One'* of several deep, dark places in his journey.

But as he always did, because of God's favor, Joseph flourished anyway. He landed feet-first in the house of Potiphar, captain of Pharaoh's palace guard. Good things began to happen. Potiphar prospered with this smart, poised Hebrew in-residence. Joseph soon accumulated well-earned authority and responsibility. His godly character and values served him well in business, as many have found in the workplace. He proved his master's confidence well placed and gained Potiphar's complete trust. Joseph had reached improbable *'Mountaintop Number Two.'*

As his journey accelerated

### BTW

- **JOSEPH** was his father's favorite son, firstborn of Jacob's beloved wife, Rachel. Jacob worked seven years for her hand, only to be cheated by her father.

- He had eleven brothers. Only one of the brothers was Rachel's son.

- Being Jacob's favorite, Joseph was hated by his second-class brothers. So much so that they were willing to do anything to be rid of him.

- They threw him into a dry well in a remote place, planning to kill him later. Then an opportunity arose, and they sold him to traders from Midian.

- Eventually he was resold to one of Pharaoh's Egyptian officials, rebuffed sexual advances from the man's wife, and ended up in prison.

- Finally, he became Pharaoh's right-hand man.

- **THE LESSON:** Obeying God and holding onto your values will please God and optimize your future. Anything is possible with God.

and the road smoothed out, the handsome young man caught the eye of Potiphar's wife, and potholes developed on his smooth ride. As he began his descent into *'Valley Number Two,'* the woman pursued him relentlessly. He found himself fending off her unwanted sexual advances. We might think it was simply his fear of rocking the pleasant boat he was riding, but the Scripture reveals a more altruistic reasoning in Joseph's heart. When she came on to him, he refused. "With me in charge," he told her, "My master does not concern himself with anything in the house. Everything he owns he has entrusted to my care. No one is greater in this house than I am. My master has withheld nothing from me except you, because you are his wife. How then could I do such a wicked thing and **sin against God**?"

If Joseph had complied with her demand for sex, by today's common reasoning he might have enhanced his long–term career chances. But he rightly identified the target of such an offense—*God?*" His focus was higher even than the employer who trusted him. God would feel the sting of adultery. So, how could such a "success" bring such an affront to God? Good question!

Can we even imagine the temptation he felt? Who could hardly blame Joseph if he rationalized away his boyhood faith? "God doesn't seem to be taking very good care of me. In fact, I don't even know if God's power extends to this part of the world.

"I guess I'm on my own in life now. I have to look out for my own interests. No one else will take care of me. I'm light years from home. Who will even know if I embrace a new moral code? Giving in to adultery might open new doors of opportunity. Faithfulness doesn't seem to be working too well."

The possible rationalizations are endless: how easy it is to give in, how hard it is to stay true to godly values. If we didn't know better, we might think Joseph lived in the twenty–first century. The stresses, the tempting shortcuts, the copouts seem so...*today*. As I read Joseph's story,

I almost expected to discover that his world included *The Washington Post* or CNN. That's how similar many elements in his world were to what we see every day, all around us. And so many are caving in to the pressures. But if Joseph were here now, I think he'd stand up under the temptations. He'd reject the rationalizations that place blame elsewhere, looking for the easy way out. What a man he would be in today's pressure-cooker world. A man to admire, a man to emulate.

So, this young man of integrity found that his faithfulness landed him in prison for the crime of not knuckling under to wickedness. There he was, stumbling around in the gloomy shadows of Valley Number Two.

But not for long. They say the cream always rises to the top. Sure enough, Joseph was soon promoted from convict to trustee to warden's helper to right-hand-man, and finally, yes, **the inmate was running the prison!** In the most improbable event yet in Joseph's roller-coaster journey through life, he earned trust and confidence once more. Can you see a trend here? From 'Valley Number Two,' the man quickly rose to *'Mountaintop Number Three.'* And God left His fingerprints all over the picture.

Psalm 105:17–19 explains, God "sent a man before them— Joseph, sold as a slave. They bruised his feet with shackles, his neck was put in irons, till what he foretold came to pass, till **the word of the Lord proved him true.**" Looking at Joseph's life from this side of the calendar, it's easy to see that God was steadily and purposefully moving Joe toward an Everest-top blessing. But the poor guy didn't have the benefit of forty centuries of insights and analysis, as we do. He was up to his cowlick in the moment, and staying faithful was no doubt a second-by-second challenge.

Joseph's ultimate rise to power was so unlikely that if I included it in a proposal for the next great American novel, some sharp editor would probably throw the manuscript on the reject pile, shake her head and say,

"Nobody would ever believe that storyline. It's just too farfetched." God would never make it as an acquisitions editor on Publisher's Row.

After Joseph accessed God's power to correctly interpret two dreams, and after being forgotten until God's timing was perfect (*'Valley Number Three'*), Joseph ultimately rose to power in so unexpected a way that it could only have been a God Thing. Ultimate faithfulness and obedience became ultimate power, as Joseph sat on a throne only inches below Pharaoh's. That throne was perched high on *'Mountaintop Number Four.'*

> **When life serves up lemons, it's just good business to open a lemonade stand.**

Just in case you have your eye on becoming Prime Minister, remember that God likely has a different plan for you than He did for Joseph. But His plan for you also begins with faithfulness and obedience. God always plans to use women and men who put faithfulness and obedience to Him ahead of any other consideration.

**Reap the results of faithfulness.** In his own words, Pharaoh assured Joseph, "You shall oversee my palace, and all my people are to submit to your orders. Only with respect to the throne will I be greater than you" (Genesis 41:40). Through the young man's leadership, the people carefully stewarded seven years of plenty and rode it to survival during the seven years of famine that followed.

The principle here is as timeless as God Himself. The ups–and–downs of Joseph's life were under the wise, loving management of God. The bad times came, and Joseph had a choice. Wait for God to organize all the ducks in a sensible row; or reject God for all the terrible things that happened, and never even notice the ducks falling into formation, as God had ordered.

When Jacob, their father died, the brothers crawled to Joseph, expecting him to take revenge for their treachery. But by then Joseph understood the valleys and mountaintops his life had included. He told them, "You meant to harm me, but God intended it all for good. He brought me to this time and place so I could save many people's lives" (Genesis 50:20).

## YOUR JOURNEY

No one is more guilty of trying to manipulate life's valleys than I. When life gave me lemons, I didn't open a lemonade stand. A refreshing iced drink never crossed my mind. Instead, I threw those lemons at the villains, turned them to a pulp under my heel, or, at best, tried to prop up the furniture with them. Most of the valley residences in my life have been wasted trying to negotiate my own advantage. I have attempted to make them something they were not, instead of simply allowing God the time and space to use them, as Joseph did—as He intended. I could cry thinking how much better my life would be if I had learned this principle many years ago.

**Endure life's valleys and mountaintops.** Surely your journey through life has had its ups and downs. No one I know has had a straight, smooth road directly to their desired destination. I couldn't begin to list your possible valleys or mountaintops. Each of us has a myriad of possibilities, and our circumstances are so individual.

We all should expect detours, speed bumps, potholes, maybe even life–altering tragic circumstances, as Joseph experienced.

**Are you faithless or faithful?** Some of these deep, dark valleys are caused by our own poor choices, our disobedience. But even people who hold onto their godly values and biblical morals and ethics experience journeys into the dark dales of life.

I believe in this inherent truth: ***It's not the low places themselves, but our response to God in those valleys, that determines our destiny.*** When you enter valleys not of your making, do you remain faithful to God? Or do you turn away from your trust and obedience? When your journey descends into darkness and gloom, do you hold onto your biblical values or do you rationalize your ungodly behavior?

**View the big picture.** On this exciting, frustrating, hopeful, fearful journey, are you able to keep the big picture in view? Do you keep trusting God even when you cannot see the big picture? Life is so 'daily,' it's often difficult to focus on the big picture.

As a new resident of Florida, I grasped what a former boss used to say. "When you're up to your [armpits] in alligators," she would quip, "it's hard to remember that the objective is to drain the swamp."

Christ is a wonderful example of someone who never let secondary things become primary. He always remembered His purpose for being here and didn't allow temptations of power or physical appetite to distract Him. As Stephen Covey has so famously said, "The main thing is to keep the main thing the main thing."[2]

Joseph never let his troubles, temptations or appetites cloud his vision of the primary priority. Even when he didn't know what God intended, or how the twisting road ahead would lead to God's will for him, he trusted God and stayed on–target.

**God keeps His promises.** Three men from California were driving to the Promise Keepers event in Washington D.C. back in 1997. As they left town, they passed a homeless man holding a "Please Help" sign. They pulled over and talked to him. He had left his family in Alabama sixteen years before and hadn't seen them since. He was now homeless and destitute. The men invited him to go to Washington with them.

He said he wasn't worthy of going to stand with so many other men to honor God. They challenged him by confessing that, although they hadn't physically abandoned their families, they had failed in other ways. They said the main reasons for going were repentance and reconciliation. This convinced him to go along for the ride.

As they approached the Capital Mall in Washington D.C., they said perhaps they could find a group from Alabama so he could talk with

---

[2] The Main Thing – The Resicom Group (https://resicomonline.com/building-somthing-great)

men from his home state. He was skeptical. With half a million men in attendance, there was little chance of finding men from "The Heart of Dixie."

The first group they approached was from—you guessed it—Alabama. One of the Alabama men asked what town the homeless man was from. He named the place and learned that there was a man in their group from there.

When the other man from that village in Alabama was introduced, he turned out to be—you guessed it—the homeless man's son! The two spent the day together in prayer, repentance, and reconciliation, and the father ended up being reunited with his family.

What a journey! Not just for the homeless man and his son, but for the men from California whom God directed on a special cross-country journey with a wonderful mountaintop destination.

---

**MOMENT OF TRUTH**

When life's journey takes you through dark, dangerous valleys, stay true to your biblical values. God is waiting there to lead you out of the valley to the sunny mountaintop above.

---

**MY PERSONAL JOURNEY:** One time that I lost my way in a dark valley was:

_____

_____

_____

_____

_____

- One time that I held onto godly values in a time of potential compromise was:

_____

- I am going through a dark valley right now ☐ yes ☐ no. Explain…

- The godly morals and ethics I need to hold onto in this valley are:

- With God's help, I'm going to make a journey through this valley and emerge exactly where God wants me to be. Here's how:

**This YouTube video reveals great truth about Joseph's timeless story:**
If You Want Me To - Ginny Owens | With Lyrics

# 3
# LOVE'S LONG JOURNEY

**JOURNEY TO TRUE LOVE**
— Ruth and Naomi —
(Ruth 1–4)

### TRUE LOVE RISKED

In his *Stories from Around the World*,[3] Lafcadio Hearn told of a Japanese fishing village where an earthquake rattled the villagers one evening. Being accustomed to such temblors, they soon went back to their activities. Behind the village, on the steep slope overlooking the ocean, a prosperous old farmer stood watching the sea. He thought the water looked strange and dark, moving against the wind, flowing away from the shore. He knew the signs—a tsunami would crash ashore directly, destroying everything in its path, because the earthquake had occurred offshore, under the sea floor.

The farmer called to his grandson, "Hurry! Bring me a torch." Behind his house lay his great crop of rice, ready for the trip to market. And it was worth a fortune—one of his best crops ever. In just a moment,

---

[3] This story grew out of the December 23, 1854 Nankai earthquake (8.4 magnitude) and tsunami. • https://etc.usf.edu/lit2go/pdf/passage/5221/stories-from-around-the-world-004-the-burning-of-the-rice-fields.pdf

his torch set great heaps of grain and rice straw on fire. Then, from the village temple below, a bell began to peal—"Fire!"

Up the mountain from the seaside village streamed all the people. They were coming to put out the terrible consuming fire. "He's mad!" they screamed when they saw the old farmer applying the torch to his precious harvest.

Then he pointed out to sea and shouted, "Look!" At the edge of the horizon they saw a long, thin line of water that thickened even as they watched. It was the sea, rising into a great wall and thundering down on the village more swiftly than a diving eagle. Then came the shock, heavier even than the earthquake itself. The great wall of water struck the shore with a blow that made the hills tremble. It tore through their homes like matchsticks. It drew back, roared in again…and again…and again. Finally, it slowed, then ebbed, then returned to its place.

On the bluff, no one spoke a word. Then they heard the old man say softly, "That is why I set fire to the rice. I knew you would all run up here and be safe from the tsunami."

He stood among them, once the wealthiest man of the village, now impoverished. But he had saved the lives of his family and friends. They were his relatives, though maybe not in the strictest sense. But to him, they were family, and they were worth more than any crop of rice. Love makes people do extraordinary things.

A few verses in Ruth chapter one have been used innumerable times in countless wedding ceremonies to illustrate the depth of true love. But most people never think much about the fact that the love story found there is not about a man and a woman—or even about a woman and her mother. The story of Ruth and Naomi begins as a love story between a widow and her foreign-born, widowed daughter-in-law. Not your run-of-the-mill "Hallmark Channel" love story. But it provides a powerful reminder that love for family may send us on the journey of a lifetime!

## TRUE LOVE REVEALED

**She did it all for love.** In Ruth chapter one, the father and two sons died, leaving behind their destitute widows, mother Naomi, and the two Moabite daughters–in–law, Orpah and Ruth. When Naomi tried to send them back to their father's homes, Orpah wept, kissed Naomi, and turned back to her old life. Ruth, on the other hand, was not so easily dismissed. She clung to this foreigner she had come to love so much.

"Look," said Naomi, "your sister–in–law is going back to her people and her gods. Go back with her."

But Ruth replied, "Don't urge me to leave you or to turn back from you. Where you go I will go, and where you stay I will stay. Your people will be my people and your God my God. Where you die I will die, and there I will be buried. May the Lord deal with me, be it ever so severely, if even death separates you and me" (Ruth 1:15–17).

True love has the power to demolish social and cultural barriers. Ruth was from Moab, a nation despised by the people of Israel—and vice versa. Moab's founder and namesake was the son of Abraham's nephew Lot, and Lot's own daughter. That's right, Moab was the product of drunken incest (Genesis 19:31–38). This alone would have been enough to make Moab and its people despised by Hebrews like Naomi and her husband. Throughout the Old Testament, Moab and Israel were sworn enemies.

The love of a Moabite daughter–in–law for her Israelite mother–in–law was outlandishly unexpected. A love like this says something about the depth of the relationships in this biblical family. Ruth had a family of origin in Moab, one to which she could return, since her husband, an Israelite alien, had died. The common expectation was that Ruth would stay in her native country when Naomi returned to Bethlehem.

It was customary for a young woman whose husband died to return to her father's house and await another suitor. The widow often became a 'second' wife, more convenience, more "work mule" than a cherished, beloved partner. Opportunities were not necessarily great and the prospects were not always inviting, but that's the way life was in the Mideast more than a thousand years before Christ.

With Naomi's departure at hand, Ruth and Orpah accompanied her to the outskirts of town, where she did her best to send them back to their fathers' care. Orpah cried and wailed, then turned back to her own people, her gods, and her hometown. But Ruth's decision to leave Moab and make the long journey with Naomi over dangerous, barren mountains to Bethlehem was a strange one indeed. It violated all the customs of that day and place. Ruth loved her mother–in–law so much that she would rather undergo the arduous trip, take the risks of a dangerous journey, struggle with the cross–cultural adjustments of a new home, and leave her own father and mother behind, than be separated from the family member who had become so precious to her. Ruth epitomized the truth that **"Love builds families, and through families, God builds His Kingdom."**

The biblical Orpah acted in the expected way, thinking first of her own needs, desires, and security, putting herself ahead of Naomi. This brief mention in Ruth 1:15 is the last the world heard of Orpah. But because of her selfless act of devotion, Ruth has been a symbol of unselfish, devoted love for three thousand years. She modeled a depth of love that's the perfect example for all kinds of relationships from that day to this.

**Love changes everything.** Ruth showed us that love can embrace all areas of life. "…Don't urge me to leave you or to turn back from you. Where you *go* I will go, and where you *stay* I will stay. Your *people* will be my people and your *God* my God. Where you *die* I will die, and there I will be *buried*. May the Lord deal with me, be it ever so severely, if anything but death separates you and me" (Ruth 1:16, 17, italics added).

Ruth said, "I'm willing to make a complete life–change, because of my love for you. I'd rather be with you than hold onto my old, familiar ways, my old home, my old beliefs." Ruth's decision to follow the love of her heart meant she would be adjusting to many new things—new family members, new customs, a new home, and new religious beliefs. She would be cutting all ties with the old ways, the old life. That's what family love means—sacrificing and risking everything else to bless those God has placed in our families. **It means, "This love is the very air that I breathe!"**

John R. W. Stott, famous pastor of London's All Souls Church, said it like this: "God created fish to live and thrive in water, whether salt or fresh. Gills are adapted to absorb oxygen from water, so water is the element in which a fish finds its identity, its freedom, its 'fishness.' It finds itself in the element for which it was created: water. It is limited to water, but in that limitation is liberty.

"Suppose you had a little tropical fish in one of those old-fashioned, spherical goldfish bowls. Suppose the little fish swam round and round his blessed bowl until his frustration became unbearable. The fish decided to make a bid for freedom and leap out of the bowl. If it landed in a pond in your backyard, it would increase its freedom because there would be more water to swim in. But if it landed on the concrete or on the carpet, then its bid for freedom would come to a sudden end.

Stott asks, "If fish were meant for water, what are human beings made for?...What is the element in which human beings find themselves, as water is the element in which a fish finds itself?

> **Life formula: Love = (Risk$^{10}$) + Joy$^{32}$**

"I don't hesitate to say that **according to Scripture the answer is *love*. Human beings are made for love because God is love.** When he created us in his own image, he gave us the capacity to love and to be loved. So human beings find their destiny in loving God and in loving their neighbors."[4]

---

[4] John R.W. Stott, "Freedom," Preaching Today tape # 102

As Ruth's journey showed, human beings find their destiny in loving and being loved by their families. This powerful love of Ruth's for Naomi encompassed all aspects of life. After all, love is the fertile soil in which life grows and thrives. The love was worth the bother.

## TRUE LOVE REWARDED

Welcome to strange. Ruth soon learned that customs in Israel were, indeed, foreign. She went to gather grain left behind by the reapers. There she discovered that custom required the closest relative to "redeem" the lost family line by marrying the widow and fathering a child to carry on the dead husband's name. She also met the gentleman farmer, who praised her for standing by Naomi in her hour of need. Boaz said, "May you be richly rewarded by the Lord, the God of Israel, under whose wings you have come to take refuge."

By "divine coincidence," this Boaz happened to be a close relative of Naomi and figured prom-

> **BTW**
> - **Boaz** was a successful Hebrew businessman and relative of Naomi's husband, Elimelech.
> - Jewish law required the closest relative of a deceased man to marry the surviving childless widow, to continue the dead man's name.
> - Before Boaz ever knew of the family connection, he was attracted to Ruth, widow of Mahlon, Elimelech's son. When he learned of the family connection he acted at once.
> - He approached the one relative closer to Elimelech than he.
> - When the other man declined the opportunity to marry Ruth, Boaz took immediate steps to fulfill his family obligation.
> - Ruth and Boaz were the Great Grandparents of King David, the forerunner of Jesus Christ.
> - **THE LESSON:** *God has a way of turning obligations into blessings. Boaz married Ruth to fulfill the law, but gained a loving wife. They blessed humankind from that day to this.*

inently in the whole scheme of redemption. Of course, there is no such thing as "divine coincidence." For the Christian, I'm not sure there is such a thing as "coincidence" of any kind. If you believed in coincidence, you could believe that Ruth just "happened" to go into Boaz's field to pick up grain behind the reapers. You could believe that Boaz just happened along and saw the eligible young widow. If you believed in coincidence, you could think they just happened to connect, by accident, in a special, God-kind of loving way. No, God was at work in this story, and so Ruth's journey was guided, unknown to her, by God's hand. Each detail of her blissfully unaware journey was being orchestrated by God to achieve His own eternal purposes.

This was the beginning of a match made in heaven. The girl who journeyed the dangerous, uncertain road out of love for her mother-in-law was about to get an even greater love. Neither Ruth nor Boaz knew the other existed, but God knew. He arranged the circumstances to bring the two together in a barley field. It was the eternal workings of the God of the universe.

**True love was in full flower.** Ruth came to Bethlehem out of love for Naomi, but God was not done with 'love' in Ruth's life. Because of her honorable actions, Boaz took care of the legalities that very same day and the marriage was consummated. Though no one could see the future, God was working the minute details of this loving marriage to accomplish His own eternal purposes. Ruth became part of Israel's rich history because she followed her heart!

The final verses of the book of Ruth list the genealogy of this remarkable love story. "Salmon the father of Boaz, Boaz the father of Obed, Obed the father of Jesse, and Jesse the father of David" (Ruth 4:21–22). Boaz was the great-grandfather of King David, and Ruth, the Gentile foreign-born Moabite woman, was David's great-grandmother. Ruth became a distant ancestor of Jesus Christ, Son of God, Savior of the world! A love story too magnificent to be featured on "Hallmark Channel.®"

## TRUE LOVE REPEATED

**God has His own family.** "Because of the Lord's great love we are not consumed, for his compassions never fail. They are new every morning; great is your faithfulness" (Lamentations 3:22, 23). The love so beautifully displayed in Ruth's story was lived, from distant eons past, by God Himself.

Ruth's journey offered a hint of the journey made to earth by the Son of God, out of love for this human family to which we belong. It was a journey filled with danger and risk and trouble. It climaxed in rescue for all who trust in Him as Savior—all who love Him. God's love is repeated every time one of us lives out the love of God in real life. And God expresses His love for us through family. "God sets the lonely in families..." (Psalm 68:6).

Today, we see the love of God pictured in the family relationships we have. Not all family relationships are positive, healing, and redemptive, but God intends them to be. Too often, we self-centered humans mess them up. But the family is what God has created for the very purpose of lavishing His own love upon us.

God created us to thrive in families. It's no accident that Ruth's love for family (in her case, in-laws) instructs us today. God plans that our greatest successes, our greatest victories, are to be celebrated in the context of family. He plans that our most painful and humiliating defeats are to be cushioned by those same loving family members.

**Welcome to church as family.** God has, in fact, modeled the Christian church after the imperfect yet loving, forgiving, healing, consoling, and encouraging family. Ultimately, God intends us to be loving, forgiving, healing, consoling, encouraging members of human and divine families. ***We* are God's plan to heal the hurts, bind the bruises, give**

**guidance, celebrate the joys, and commemorate the victories of those in our human families and in His heavenly family, the church.** For those willing to make this vital journey of family love, the rewards are heavenly.

In his autobiography, *Up From Slavery*,[5] Booker T. Washington wrote, "The most trying ordeal that I was forced to endure as a slave boy...was the wearing of a flax shirt. In the portion of Virginia where I lived it was common to use flax as part of the clothing for slaves. That part of the flax from which our clothing was made was largely the refuse, which of course was the cheapest and roughest part. I can scarcely imagine any torture, except, perhaps, the pulling of a tooth, that is equal to that caused by putting on a new flax shirt for the first time. It is almost equal to the feeling that one would experience if he had a dozen or more chestnut burrs, or a hundred small pinpoints, in contact with his flesh. Even to this day, I can recall accurately the tortures that I underwent when putting on one of these garments. The fact that my flesh was soft and tender added to the pain. But I had no choice. I had to wear the flax shirt or none; and had it been left to me to choose, I should have chosen to wear no covering.

"In connection with the flax shirt, my brother John, who is several years older than I am, performed one of the most generous acts that I ever heard of one slave relative doing for another. On several occasions when I was being forced to wear a new flax shirt, he generously agreed to put it on in my stead and wear it for several days, till it was 'broken in.'"

"Brotherly love" must be what drove John to break in Booker's flax shirts. What other motivation could there be than love? This exemplified a kind of family love that Ruth well–understood. And it made an impression on the younger Booker T. Washington that stayed with him for the rest of his life.

---

[5] Booker T. Washington · Flax · Omeka S (www.psu.edu)

What kind of family love actions have we performed for our loved ones? Have you done anything in the spirit of John Washington? Is there a journey of family love you need to begin today?

> **MOMENT OF TRUTH**
> For the love of family (biological and/or spiritual), no journey is too long, too risky or too costly!

**MY PERSONAL JOURNEY:** I have recently benefited from the love of family in this way:

_____
_____
_____
_____
_____

- I could make _____'s journey better by:

_____
_____
_____
_____

- This graph describes my commitment to family love:

| 0 | 1 | 2 | 3 | 4 | 5 | 6 | 7 | 8 | 9 | 10 |
|---|---|---|---|---|---|---|---|---|---|----|
| Make no sacrifices | | | | | Certain sacrifices | | | | | Make any sacrifice |

- If I am to live out a godly kind of family love, as Ruth did, I need to set out on this journey:

_____
_____
_____
_____
_____

# 4

# THERE'S BAD NEWS, AND THERE'S GOOD NEWS

**JOURNEY TO DELIVER THE GOSPEL**
— Philip the Evangelist —
(Acts 8:1–9, 26–39)

Have you ever found yourself in a place you didn't want to be? **I found myself in Hawaii against my will, after trying everything I could think of to skip out on Paradise.** It's hard to imagine, I know, but true!

While assigned to the 101st Airborne I received orders (note: they're called 'orders' not 'suggestions') for an Army Corps of Engineers assignment in Honolulu. I could go alone and finish out the last sixteen months of my enlistment. Or I could reenlist to cover three years and take my wife and three young daughters, ages three, two, and nine months, with me. Our plans were to go to Bible College after the Army, then into ministry. So a deployment overseas, even to Hawaii, seemed a waste of time.

I considered various actions to avoid going. Finally, with all other avenues of escape exhausted, I briefly considered going AWOL. Thankfully, I came to my senses and discarded that stupid idea. Instead, I reluctantly accepted the assignment and took my young family along.

Despite my grudging obedience, God blessed our three-year tropical journey in many ways.

For Philip, a first-century believer gifted and called to the mission of spreading God's Good News, finding himself in Gaza (yes, *that* Gaza) was the result of bad news and good news. **The bad news** was that persecution plagued the fledgling church. **The good news** was that the **bad news propelled the Good News** beyond Jerusalem into a dark world aching for healing from its soul sickness.

## HARDSHIP WAS THE GARDEN PLOT FOR CHRISTIANITY

**Radical change followed on the heels of tragedy.** Stephen the Deacon was killed for his witness about Jesus (Acts chapter 7). The Christians in Jerusalem were then scattered throughout the region. This became the new mission field for the Good News. The faithful but harassed Christians of Acts chapter 8 preached the good news everywhere they went.

"**The blood of the martyrs is the seed of the church**" is an historical description of this bad news–good news contrast, likely articulated by the second century church father, Tertullian.

> Opposition has spread Christianity to the far corners of God's green earth.

Speaking of martyrs, *Christianity Today* magazine says **seventy-million people have died for their faith** since Jesus walked the earth.[6] The International Institute for Religious Freedom estimated between 4,000 and 6,000 Christians were killed for their faith in 2017. The *Christian Post* reports that **4,761 Christians lost their lives in 2020, strictly to religious persecution.** The Vatican News website says an average of **thirteen believers die every day** because of their Christian beliefs. Additionally, a dozen Christians are unjustly arrested or imprisoned and five are kidnapped each day.[7]

---

[6] www.appgfreedomofreligionorbelief.org
[7] www.vaticannews.va

**Cultural indifference became official government persecution.** As a result of oppression, the church of the first century flourished and grew in the face of determined hostility. Jewish religious and political leaders were at first confused and anxious about the disciples of that troublemaker, Jesus of Nazareth. Soon, however, they got organized and presented a unified front against His followers. Their aggression forced Christians to unevangelized places across the known world. Believers on the run took their faith with them. That's good news.

Christ followers in Rome were mostly ignored until Nero made them his scapegoat during the great fire of Rome (July 18, AD 64). As "punishment" for nonexistent crimes, Nero waged a sustained pogrom against them and his atrocities were horrible. One grisly example has Nero setting tar-coated Christians afire as torches to illuminate his garden party orgies.[8]

Illogically, persecution of the church has hastened its spread and growth. For two thousand years, **the bad-news harassment of God's people has resulted in the advancement of the Good News.** From twelve apostles and a few hundred followers in the first century, the church has grown to about 2.38 billion believers.[9]

I had the privilege of traveling to China and on to Tibet (pre-COVID-19). Our group of ten made a prayer journey in the so-called "10/40 Window"[10] to one of the most mysterious places on earth. Tibet remains one of the least-evangelized regions, where the Good News has made limited headway against "the powers of this dark world."

As our prayer group walked the streets of Lhasa and drove through the countryside, we asked God to raise up a Christian witness among

---

[8] www.eyewitnesstohistory.com
[9] www.pewresearch.org/religion/2011/12/19/global-christianity/
[10] The 10/40 Window is the designation given to sixty-nine nations with little Christian presence, by The Joshua Project in the 1980s. It represents the rectan-gular area of North Africa, the Middle East, and Asia approximately between 10 degrees north and 40 degrees north latitude. The 10/40 Window includes the ma-jority of the world's Muslims, Hindus and Buddhists.

the Chinese authorities and the local populace. With that prayer came the stunning thought that the phrase, "The blood of the martyrs is the seed of the church," probably applied to any Christian awakening in Tibet. In reality, we were praying for a movement that would be accompanied by blood, fire and tears. How sobering!

## PHILIP'S CALLING TO TAKE A GOSPEL JOURNEY

**An angel sent the Evangelist off on a divine mission.** The holy messenger told him, "Go south to the road (ὁδός–hodos· *road, way, avenue for a journey*) that goes down from Jerusalem to Gaza." God's call included specific instructions. This journey teaches Christ followers never to ignore God's call to publicize the Good News. But make sure you get your signals straight. If you feel reluctant to obey, like Moses at the burning bush, it may actually be a sign of God's true call.

In contrast, I've learned to be cautious when God's will seems to align perfectly with my own. It's never easy to separate what I want from God's actual will for me. Once God has confirmed His calling in your life, hit the pavement running!

**Philip followed the road God put before him.** As he obeyed God and set off on the road from Jerusalem to Gaza on the seacoast, he met a government official from Ethiopia. After worshiping the Jewish God in Jerusalem, he was returning home. As he read Isaiah's prophecy of the Messiah in chapter 53, the Holy Spirit told Philip to approach him. In order for God's plan to succeed, Philip had to engage with the Ethiopian man. **Evangelism always includes connection.**

So, he ran up to him and asked, "Do you understand what you're reading?" In response, he asked Philip to explain the passage. Subsequently, the man believed in Jesus, was baptized, and began celebrating his newfound faith. Unexpectedly, the Spirit of the Lord then mysteriously removed the Evangelist from the scene and the new believer resumed his journey homeward, rejoicing as he went. The incident re-

## THERE'S BAD NEWS, AND THERE'S GOOD NEWS

sulted, historically, in a growing church in Africa. Today, the Coptic Church attests to this amazing event, spawned by Philip's obedient journey to proclaim the Good News.

**"If you want things to change, tell someone about Jesus."** So says Discipleship Pastor Kenny Tibbetts, of First Baptist Church, Palmetto, FL.[11] Combined with the saying (maybe you've seen the bumper sticker), **"Be the change you want to see,"** our personal responsibility to spread the Good News about Jesus is emphasized.

There are people who claim to be Christians for the perceived personal benefits they want. Often, **these people are reluctant, even unwilling, to make substantive changes in how they live.** Just the fact you're reading this book suggests you're not one of them. Someone has quoted Ann Lamott saying, "God loves you just the way you are, but He loves you too much to leave you just the way you are."[12]

### BTW

- **The Ethiopian Eunuch** was an official in the court of Queen Candace.

- Ethiopia is in northeast Africa. The Blue Nile River arises in northern Ethiopia.

- The Eunuch had been castrated, perhaps signaling an effort to improve his focus on one area of responsibility, to the elimination of certain distractions.

- The Eunuch was apparently a seeker after the God of the Old Testament, a proselyte of the religion of Judaism.

- He was confused as he read Isaiah 53, known as the "Suffering Servant" passage. Philip explained it from his "Jesus is Messiah" perspective. The man then put his trust in Jesus as Savior and was baptised.

- **THE LESSON:.** *God is looking for followers in the most unexpected places. Jesus is Savior of everyone who seeks Him. Never underestimate who might want to know Christ. The Good News is for everyone.*

---

[11] From a message by Rev. Kenny Tibbetts, June 12, 2023, FBCPalmetto FL
[12] https://salvagedfaith.com/2016/01/19

**Faith without willingness to change is empty.** It's akin to James's words about faith and works. "What good is it, dear brothers and sisters, if you say you have faith but don't show it by your actions? Can that kind of faith save anyone?" (James 2:14 NLT).

## CONNECT TO PASS ALONG THE GOOD NEWS

**Philip was in the right place at the right time.** During the first century AD, angels seemed more likely to talk verbally to Christians than they are today. We have the essential message of hope, inspired by God, recorded in the Bible. In Philip's day, not so much. Though the fledgling New Testament was in the making, Philip's Scriptures still consisted of just the Old Testament.

Admittedly, our Bible doesn't give us specific guidance for individual circumstances, such as the angel gave Philip in Acts chapter 8. Yet, there are plenty of stories from people who've heard from God about what they are to do. Philip's instructions included what road to take, which person to approach once he got there and even what to say to the Ethiopian. Philip had to **obey one instruction before he received the next. That's a common principle for finding and doing God's will**. Obey the orders you have; don't wait for the complete picture to develop.

Have you ever asked God to set up 'divine appointments' in order to guide you in your interactions? I believe many people want you to share Jesus with them. They just don't know that's what they want. They may only realize it when you obey God.

I wonder what Philip was thinking when he arrived on the Jerusalem–Gaza road and saw an African government official riding in a chariot, reading a scroll. Do you suppose he said to himself, "Hey, that guy's reading the Bible and wants me to interpret it for him"? Maybe not. But he obeyed what he understood God's instructions to be—**he connected with the man.** What he discovered was a convert to Judaism wrestling with Isaiah's prophecy about Jesus, the Suffering Servant.

"Do you understand what you're reading?" Philip asked. A logical question and about as non-threatening as you can get. When the Ethiopian admitted he did not and asked for Philip's help, the process of evangelism unfolded, a new Christian was born, and Philip's journey to share the Good News moved forward.

**Ask a simple question.** Often, all it takes is the right question to uncover a heart searching for God. In his book *Share Jesus Without Fear*[13], Bill Fay suggests a series of brief questions that build one upon the other. Proceed to the next only if there is implied consent.

1. Do you have any spiritual belief?
2. To you, who is Jesus?
3. Do you believe there is a heaven and a hell?
4. If you died right now, where would you go? If heaven, why?
5. If what you believe were not true, would you want to know it?

If the person says 'yes' to question 5, open your Bible. (Fay offers several Scriptures that explain the plan of salvation.) If, at any point, the individual seems unwilling to go forward, simply stop. Remember, **it's the Holy Spirit's job to draw unbelievers to faith, not yours.** If you simply obey God by interacting, you cannot fail. Now, there's a good definition of 'success.'

**God's Word changes hearts.** With Isaiah's prophecy explained, the Ethiopian's heart was melted and he embraced Jesus Christ as God's anointed Messiah. If you're sincere about bringing change, then tell someone about Jesus. God's Word is the script. Be sure you are prepared, prayed up, and equipped with good resources for the seeker. Don't ever suppose that Satan will allow such evangelizing without fighting back—be prepared!

Finally, trust God for results from your obedience. It's never your job to change anyone—you can't. Only God can do that. But He has a

---

[13] Fay, William and Linda Evans Shepherd, 1999. Share Jesus Without Fear. Nashville: B&H Publishing Group

part for you to play in others' heart change.

Telling others about Jesus involves a journey that frightens many, and excites others. It's the devil who instills and inflates fear. But you're not called to 'save' anyone, only to connect with them and be a resource God will use in the process.

Offer yourself to God on this journey. Simply obey Him, and let the fireworks begin. You have nothing to lose but fear itself.

> **MOMENT OF TRUTH**
> Ask God to connect you with people who are open to the Good News. He alone can save them, but He wants to involve you.

**MY PERSONAL JOURNEY:** Let me tell about a time I found myself in a place God had sent me that I didn't want to be:

_____
_____
_____
_____
_____

- When I am faced with a witnessing opportunity, my first thought is:
_____
_____
_____
_____

- Here are my thoughts on Philip's journey to share the Good News about:

# THERE'S BAD NEWS, AND THERE'S GOOD NEWS

+ How easily Philip knew about about what to do next:
_____
_____

+ How everything fell into place for Philip to share the Good News:
_____
_____

+ How Philip interacted, but it was God who saved the man:
_____
_____

- Here's how I rank myself on the journey to share the Gospel:

| 0 | 1 | 2 | 3 | 4 | 5 | 6 | 7 | 8 | 9 | 10 |
|---|---|---|---|---|---|---|---|---|---|----|

I never share      A mix of success and failure      I thrive on sharing Good News

- Lord help me do the following on my journey to share Jesus without fear:
_____
_____
_____
_____
_____

# 5

# ROADMAP TO PEACE

### JOURNEY TO MAKE HARMONY
— Abigail —
1 Samuel 25

### FIND AND LISTEN TO YOUTUBE: HE IS OUR PEACE– MARANATHA! SINGERS

The expression, "roadmap to peace" describes an effort to bring peace to Israel and the Mideast during the George W. Bush administration. A *USA Today* story described a visit to the Texas White House by then–Israeli Prime Minister Ariel Sharon. The President urged him to stop escalating Jewish settlement in Palestinian territory. Such expansion would, in Bush's opinion, throw up a roadblock to Israel's journey to peace. The President's roadmap offered a route to get Israelis out of areas being handed over to the Palestinians. This plan ostensibly provided principles that would usher in an era of Middle East peace. In hindsight, events from October 7, 2023 and beyond cast doubt upon the efficacy of Bush's "roadmap."

One Old Testament story includes its own roadmap to peace. The account involves soon–to–be King David and a capable, accomplished woman who was determined to champion peace. She tackled conflict resolution when confronted by the prospect of terrible destruction to life and limb.

## THE CONFLICT

**Two sides were spoiling for a fight.** A wealthy Israelite farmer during King Saul's reign, Nabal, had a beautiful, godly wife. In the local dialect, Nabal meant *fool* or *folly*. He was infamous for his malice. His default settings were insult and cruelty. His wife was Abigail. Foolish husband. Wise wife.

Nabal's field hands pastured and sheared his sheep in a rural area where Israel's future King David was on maneuvers with about four hundred loyal men.

While David's ragtag volunteer army was camped near Nabal's hired hands, they shielded them and their livestock from mischief. The paramilitary group protected the farm workers from harm. They treated them civilly. They helped preserve harmony for Nabal's shepherds and shearers. They safeguarded "the fool's" property. It wasn't unexpected to receive some kind of repayment for helping Nabal. So, David respectfully requested whatever the wealthy farmer would be willing to give to keep his troops fed.

> **You don't have to be a Beatnik to join the peace march started long, long ago!**

Nabal was not obligated to give anything. He could have courteously declined the request. But he was incapable of polite refusal. He could not curb his spitefulness. His contrary nature showed through.

"Who is this David?" he sneered. "Who is this son of Jesse? Many servants are running away from their masters these days. Why should I take my bread and water and the meat I have slaughtered for my shearers, and give it to this band of outlaws?" He answered David's friendly gesture with contempt. His response reflected his character: insolent, arrogant, hostile.

And so, the peace was shattered. The bucolic countryside sizzled with tension. Upon hearing Nabal's arrogant reply, David and his men strapped on their weapons, ready to defend their honor. The Bible doesn't comment about the morality of David's response. Neither sanction nor condemnation. But one thing was certain: the conflict was about to draw blood. The peace David had preserved in the fields was evaporating like the morning dew.

## THE CONFLICT RESOLUTION

Know the nitty gritty. Details of the conflict soon emerged. A servant of Nabal's explained to Abigail that David's men had protected the field hands from thieves and other mischief while they were away from home. He pleaded with Abigail to intervene before blood was spilled. He observed that disaster was hanging over them all, because Nabal was "so ill-tempered that no one can even reason with him."

Sometimes, the peace is threatened because we don't accurately understand the problem. The oper-

> **BTW**
> - **Polygamy.** The Old Testament is full of men with multiple wives. In modern western society, this practice is outlawed.
> - Single women were almost always dependent on men for their livelihoods and safety. Only a few examples of independently wealthy women appear in Scripture (ie., Proverbs 31).
> - Stability, safety, companionship, economic resources, reproduction and political alliances are all cited as cultural reasons for polygamy in ancient times. In 2022, there were 4–billion men, to 3.95 billion women in the world.
> - 1 Cor. 7 encouraged monogamy to avoid rampant immorality in the 1st century A.D.
> - Polygamy was not God's best plan, nor did He outlaw it. But both testaments uphold monogamy as the norm.
> - **THE LESSON:** *The Bible reports many cases of polygamy, but never endorses nor sanctions it.*

ative principle is to make sure you understand the conflict correctly. The Nabal–David conflict was clearly explained to Abigail, and she immediately knew what to do.

The Bible says she wasted no time. She did not waver with indecision. She knew that making no decision would actually be a disastrous decision. Quickly, Abigail decided to go on a peace march. She devised a strategy and developed the tactics needed to defuse the explosive state of affairs. She gathered bread, wine, mutton, roasted grain, figs, and raisins. She loaded beasts of burden and sent them ahead on the route David and his men were likely to follow.

To make peace, Abigail needed to understand human nature and behavioral theory. She perceived the volatile emotions of those involved. She even used her knowledge of geography to find the attackers. She perceived, however, that one more thing was necessary. She took active measures to appease the anger and lower the temperature of the two opposing sides.

First Lady Eleanor Roosevelt once said, "It isn't enough to talk about peace. One must believe in it. And it isn't enough to believe in it. One must work at it."[14] Henri Nouwen, the Dutch Catholic Priest and philosopher, said, "In a world so torn apart by rivalry, anger, and hatred, we have the privileged vocation to be living signs of a love that can bridge all divisions and heal all wounds."[15]

David had just been telling his troops, "A lot of good it did to help this wicked fellow Nabal. We protected his flocks in the wilderness, and nothing he owned was lost or stolen. But he has repaid me evil for good. May God strike me and kill me if even one man of his household is still alive in the morning!"

---

[14] Eleanor Roosevelt - It isn't enough to talk about peace.... (brainyquote.com) • www.brainyquote.com/quotes/eleanor_roosevelt_131302
[15] Being Living Signs of Love - Henri Nouwen • https://henrinouwen.org/meditations/living-signs-love

**Needed: one effective, take–charge leader.** Abigail was that command presence. She set out on the crucial journey to intercept David on his murderous expedition. When she found him, she bowed in deference and offered to the offended men a peace proposal. She accepted responsibility, though, in fact, she bore no blame. She hadn't even learned of the incident until afterward. But she graciously told David, "I accept blame in this matter, sir." She seemed to say, "If you feel the need to blame someone, I have broad shoulders." Next, she thanked God that He had kept the offended troops from acting in uncontrolled rage. She injected moral and ethical principles into the equation.

Then she pointed to the peace offering she had sent. "Please accept this present for yourself and your young men." Abigail was more generous than she had to be. Generosity became a load–bearing pillar in the peace process. She observed that God would reward the future king with a long–lasting dynasty because he was known for fighting the Lord's battles. "Even when you are pursued by those who want to kill you, your life will be safe in God's care." Her words proved to be true.

Abigail showed respect to David; she compensated for her husband's fatal flaw. She acknowledged David's kindness and reminded him that he was a decent man. Her gifts were a true peace offering.

## PEACE PRINCIPLES FOR DAILY LIVING

Never forget God's primary place in the peace process. In his reply to Abigail's peace negotiations, David told her, "I thank God for your good sense. Bless you for keeping me from murder and carrying out vengeance on Nabal."

- **Peace Principle #1:** *Make sure you understand the conflict accurately.* Understanding the roots and issues of the conflict is vital if you hope to defuse the conflict and find common ground. Peacemaking is never a one–size–fits–all endeavor. Each situation is unique.

- **Peace Principle #2:** *God must lead in any peacemaking efforts.* David acknowledged God's hand in Abigail's journey of peace. The Scripture does not validate David's reckless actions. They are merely an element in this conflict–resolution lesson from God's Word
- **Peace Principle #3:** *Good judgment is crucial in being a peacemaker.* David identified Abigail's good judgment, as shown by her decisive actions. God wants to help us develop godly judgment.
- **Peace Principle #4:** *Put yourself in other people's shoes when mediating conflict.* Abigail looked at the conflict from David's perspective and understood the dynamics of this particular disagreement.
- **Peace Principle #5:** *Generosity is a foundation upon which peacemaking must rest.* Abigail's generosity supported reconciliation.
- **Peace Principle #6:** *Indecision is actually a disastrous decision.* Indecision and hesitation may scuttle any chance to find common ground in the heat of battle. The dynamics of conflict can change rapidly, so decisive action is crucial to success.
- **Peace Principle #7:** *Never underestimate the need for personal humility* when advancing the peace process. Pride is not only a key factor in many disagreements. It can also ambush peacemakers. Treat everyone involved with dignity, and never try to promote yourself. It's not about you. It's about finding common ground for those in disagreement. **A WORD OF CAUTION: peacemakers are not always appreciated.** If you attempt peacemaking from selfish motives, you will probably be disappointed—or worse!
- **Peace Principle #8:** *Make every effort to see conflict from the perspective of all involved.* No lasting satisfactory peace can be found if the peacemaker cannot see the conflict from all sides of the equation. This doesn't mean you have to agree with the viewpoints of any faction, but you must clearly see all sides of a dispute.
- **Peace Principle #9:** *Don't let fear paralyze you.* Take courage that peacemaking is God's will and move ahead past your anxieties.

Many attempts at peacemaking have failed because of the fear factor. The Bible says God's perfect love overcomes all fear. Anyone willing to express God's love to warring factions must ask God for the courage required to pursue peace.

- **Peace Principle #10:** *Cultivate personal righteousness as a complementary partner of peace.* There have been peacemakers who gave no thought to personal righteousness (right living according to God's word). But the most effective peacemakers nurture right living as a boost and support to peacemaking. If you want God's help to bring peace to a family, work, or church conflict, it's already established that God must play a part in the peacemaking process. Psalm 85:10 says, "righteousness and peace kiss each other."

God rewarded Abigail's journey of peace. God will always honor your efforts to pacify a conflict, even if they don't end in peace. After all, warring factions have freewill. But even partially successful or unsuccessful efforts have their compensations. Jesus taught on the hillside above the Sea of Galilee that peacemakers will be known as children of God. Often, when we practice biblical principles of peacemaking, conflict will resolve peacefully.

## THE OUTCOME

**God was accomplishing His will.** After her successful peacemaking journey, Abigail returned home, where she discovered that Nabal was celebrating his plentiful harvest with a big party. He was so drunk that she knew he wouldn't comprehend her explanation of the incident. The next morning, Nabal was sober—and no doubt hung over. When she described the whole affair, he was shocked to his core and struck by a debilitating stroke. He lingered for ten days, then died.

When he heard that Nabal was dead, David said, "Praise the Lord, who has avenged the insult I received from Nabal and has kept me from doing it myself. He has received his rightfully deserved punishment."

The story ends on a high note. David sent his messengers to Abigail, asking her to become his wife. No roses, no down-on-one-knee, no diamond engagement ring. One might question David's "romance quotient." Yet, without hesitation, she responded, "I, your servant, would be happy to marry David. I would even be willing to become a slave, washing the feet of his servants!" Humility is a prerequisite for helping others along the path to peace.

## PEACE-BREAKERS OR PEACEMAKERS?

The fourteenth-century Italian philosopher Petrarch wrote, "Five great enemies to peace are greed, ambition, envy, anger, and pride."[16] To these five, let me add one other: the sin of gossip. Proverbs says that gossip separates close friends. Like a fire without wood, a quarrel without gossip dies down.

**Gossip equals relational cancer.** The apostle Paul sounded an ominous warning in his letter to the Galatians. "If you keep on biting and devouring each other, watch out or you will be destroyed by each other."

Nothing is the enemy of peace more than backbiting gossip. It can only harm. In families and businesses, as in churches, gossip can be a cancer. Once it starts, it spreads rapidly and is more invasive than Kudzu.[17]

What does the Bible say about the subject of peace? Below are listed sixty-five verses about the Bible's teachings on peace. The word appears 249 times in the New International Version of the Old and New Testaments. Peace is a major theme in God's Word.

The Fort Worth *Star-Telegram* reported that firefighters in Genoa, Texas, were accused of deliberately setting more than 40 destructive

---

[16] Five great enemies to peace inhabit with... Petrarch - Forbes Quotes • www.forbes.com/quotes/7424/
[17] Search the Nature Conservancy website for "Kudzu: the invasive vine that ate the South"

fires. When apprehended, they explained that they had nothing to do. "We just wanted to get the red lights flashing and the bells clanging." The job of firefighters is to put out fires, not start them. Christians have a similar objective.

For God's people, a peace journey is a calling, a pursuit. God instructs us to make peace a life objective for ourselves and others. This is more than just passively liking peace in some sort of weak tea intellectual assent. This is an active, vigorous, breath–stealing dash: "Run after peace." This concept of chasing peace across the landscape is so important that David included it in Psalm 34:14. It is quoted again by the apostle Peter in 1 Peter 3:11. The two authors wrote a thousand years apart. Yet peacemaking is a timeless and timely endeavor. What greater legacy could you leave than to be a peacemaker?

---

### MOMENT OF TRUTH

The journey to peace may be long, but it's worthy of God's people to pursue such a goal. Identify situations where you can be a peacemaker, and let the journey commence!

---

**MY PERSONAL JOURNEY:** Regularly review the ten principles of peacemaking above. How do they help?

_____

_____

_____

_____

- A conflicted situation where I might be able to advance the peace process is:

_____

_____

_____

_____

_____

_____

- Read all the 'peace' verses below in one sitting.

- In addition, read and meditate on one of these passages each day. Ask God to help as you "seek peace and pursue it!"

- Using one or more of these verses, write an essay, or verbalize your beliefs about peace. Focus on a past conflict that you experienced. Ask your pastor or a trusted mentor to review it.

- Obtain a copy of Ken Sande's *The Peacemaker* for an in–depth study of the peacemaking process.

☒ What the Bible says about peace and peacemaking:

• Numbers 6:24–26; 25:12 • Judges 6:24 • Job 22:21 • Psalm 34:14; 37:37; 85:8, 10; 119:165 • Proverbs 3:2; 12:20; 16:7; 29:17 • Isaiah 9:6–7; 26:3; 27:5–6; 32:17–18 • Jeremiah 29:7 • Nahum 1:15 • John 14:27; 16:33 • Matthew 5:9 • Luke 1:79 (John the Baptist); 7:50; 8:48 • Acts 10:36 • Romans 5:1; 8:6; 12:18; 14:17, 19 • 1 Corinthians 7:15; 14:33 • 2 Corinthians 13:11 • Galatians 5:22–23 • Ephesians 2:14–17; 4:3; 6:15 • Philippians 4:4–9 • Colossians 1:19–20; 3:15 • 1 Thessalonians 5:12–13 • 1 Timothy 2:1–2 • 2 Timothy 2:22 • Hebrews 12:11, 14 • James 3:18 • 1 Peter 3:11

# 6

# NO PAIN, NO GAIN

**JOURNEY THROUGH SUFFERING**
— Job —
(Book of Job)

After working as a sports cartoonist, Charles Templeton became a Christian evangelist. He was gifted at preaching. In the 1940s, he and Billy Graham shared the platform on an evangelistic crusade across Europe. Together with Torrey Johnson, the three founded Youth for Christ International.

Someone who knew both men once said that Billy Graham was a good preacher, but Charles Templeton was the better communicator.[18] Thunderclouds troubled his horizon, however. He struggled with spiritual issues and sometimes shared his doubts with Billy. Eventually, he stopped preaching and embraced agnosticism, the belief that you cannot know if God exists. The tipping point came when he saw a magazine cover that pictured an African mother holding her dying baby. He asked why, if God was so great, He couldn't, or wouldn't, send some rain to save the dying children. He agonized over this, and finally came to believe that God does not exist. How could a loving, all-powerful God allow

---

[18] Billy Graham and Charles Templeton: The Sad Tale of Two Evangelists - Credo House Ministries • http://credohouse.org/blog/billy-graham-and-charles

such human suffering? The avowed atheist wrote the book *Farewell to God* in 1996.[19]

Late in life (Templeton died in 2001 at age 85), Billy Graham visited his old friend in Toronto. Charles had just begun his losing battle with Alzheimer's disease. He greeted the world-renowned evangelist warmly. Though rejecting the details of Jesus's teachings, he claimed to care deeply for Jesus, the man. During an interview with Lee Strobel, Templeton admitted, in tears, that he missed Jesus dreadfully.[20]

There's no doubt that Jesus missed Charles Templeton, too. His love is never-ending. But why didn't God reveal Himself to the fallen preacher? He could easily have done so. **Why does the sovereign Creator of the universe allow people not only to suffer but perhaps never to know why?** It's a mystery older than Job.

## THE MAN WHO HAD IT ALL

Some scholars believe that Moses may have written the Book of Job before he penned Genesis. Job may have been a chronological contemporary of Abraham, perhaps even older. At the very beginning of God's Self-revelation, we have this Job account about a great mystery of God's interactions with His prized creation, humankind.

**Job was a very wealthy man.** His society's scale of wealth included sheep (he had 7,000) and camels (he owned 3,000). He also had 500 teams of oxen and many other livestock. His business operations required a huge workforce just to keep up with the workload. We might picture him as the ancient equivalent of a successful major corporation CEO.

**Job was a very devoted family man.** The true measure of his success might have been his ten children. His sons were destined for future

---

[19] Templeton, Charles. 1996. Farewell to God — My Reasons for Rejecting the Christian Faith. Toronto: McLelland & Stewart, Inc.
[20] Strobel, Lee. 2000. *The Case for Faith*. Grand Rapids: Zondervan.

wealth, power, and prestige. His daughters no doubt garnered a lot of attention from eligible suitors. But mind your manners; they were surrounded by protective brothers.

When the seven sons hosted dinner parties, their sisters would join in the fun. Sometimes, the parties went on for days.

After these shindigs, Job would make sacrifices to God for them. One or more might have secretly sinned and he wanted to make sure they remained on good terms with God.

**Job was a very godly man.** The book of Job assures us that Job was "blameless and upright, a man of complete integrity." "He feared God and shunned evil." God even bragged to Satan about how righteous Job was. In fact, it was his godly character that incited the fierce testing in the first place.

Twice, God spoke to Lucifer about this blameless and upright man. The first chat, in Job chapter 1, led to the death of Job's children and the loss of his wealth at the devil's hands. The second discussion led to Satan attacking Job in person, his body covered with sores and wracked with unimaginable pain.

**He was a pillar of his community.** Job was the kind of man who chaired every social improvement committee and charity that cared for the less fortunate members of society. He fed the hungry, clothed the destitute, and housed the homeless. He even defended the innocent against their powerful oppressors.

## THE MAN WHO LOST IT ALL

**Job's wealth and family evaporated overnight.** One after the other three couriers came and reported to Job the loss of his servants and livestock. Job's empire was destroyed by a marauding band of Sabeans, fire from the sky, and Chaldean raiding parties. Finally, a fourth messenger threw the knockout punch: a tornado leveled the eldest son's house. All ten children were dead.

> **When Job had lost everything else, he held onto his faith. God rewarded him and used his example to teach generations who followed.**

The only possible chink in this ultimate family man's armor may have been Mrs. Job. When their troubles crashed ashore like a tsunami, she said to him, "Are you still maintaining your integrity? Curse God and die!" (Job 2:9). She, too, was in the grip of grief. He answered her, "You are talking like a foolish woman (the Hebrew text suggests a moral deficiency). Shall we accept good from God, and not trouble?" It was Job's godly perspective on the daunting journey ahead.

Later, Job admitted, "My breath is offensive to my wife; I am loathsome to my own family." It wasn't about halitosis. This is his commentary on the status of his life. He clung to hope that God would yet give him a measure of fairness. "Curse God? Never! Even if God kills me, my *hope* is still in Him."

When Job refused to accuse God of wrongdoing, the Lord declared to the devil, "he still maintains his integrity, though *you incited me against him to ruin him **without any reason**.*" This plays large as God resolves the whole sordid mess at the end of the book.

Four millennia later, Job's words still reverberate. "Naked I came from my mother's womb, and naked I will depart. The Lord gave and the Lord has taken away; **may the name of the Lord be praised**.' In all this, Job did not sin by charging God with wrongdoing" (Job 1:20–22).

## THE MAN WHO SUFFERED HORRIBLY

**Job suffered** *physically*. The sores that covered his body from cowlick to bunion were boils of some sort, festering and eating away at his flesh, itching, oozing, stinking, and looking repulsive.

Physical pain can be so immense that we're unable to think rationally. Most of us have never experienced such suffering; it's impossible to comprehend his pain in ordinary human terms.

**He was in anguish *mentally* and *emotionally*.** This kind of ache is, itself, able to drive people to suicide. You've probably heard stories of men who lost their fortunes on "Black Tuesday," October 29, 1929. Soon, stock market losers were plunging from the windows of upper stories, too devastated to cope with their lost wealth.

Job reeled from the loss of his wealth, even more so by the loss of his beloved children. The grief was palpable, an ache in heart and mind that threatened to sink him.

**Job agonized *spiritually*.** He could think of no sin he'd committed that should result in such terrible punishment. In Job's society, it was commonly assumed that a person never had this level of pain and anguish unless he sinned so grievously that he alienated God and brought on his own devastation. As his so-called "friends" pushed this point about sin, Job refused to acquiesce. He insisted on his innocence. He never abandoned his belief that the horrible agony was a sign of something beyond a simple penalty for grievous wrongdoing.

**Job struggled *socially*.** The friendships of Eliphaz, Bildad, and Zophar seemed to offer Job hope for support and encouragement. They remained silent in their shock and awe at his condition for seven days. Maybe they *would be* true friends. Soon, however, each, in turn, began to belabor the idea that Job had sinned wickedly against God. Repentance would fix everything, they claimed. Time after time, they accused him of infractions so out–of–character they were absurd. Job may have coined the old saying, **"With friends like you, who needs enemies?"**

Many religions strive to make sense of suffering. In Buddhism, for example, life is made up of universal suffering. Many reincarnations, with attendant *karma*, are supposedly needed to finally reach Nirvana, the Buddhist's ultimate escape from suffering by achieving 'nothingness!' Suffering is a universal conundrum to humankind.

## LESSONS ABOUT SUFFERING

A bar of steel is worth ten dollars. When cast into molded parts, it may be worth ten times that. Sharpen it into needles and its value increases to $700. If manufactured into precision parts, it's price rises exponentially to $64,000. If precision-crafted into tiny springs for high-end watches, its value skyrockets to half a million dollars. What violence that piece of steel must endure to increase its value. But the more it's shaped, formed, tempered, or cast in the crucible, the more it's worth. **You too!**

Philip Yancey says God seems to use suffering and hardship to single out the oppressed for His blessings. Jesus made statements like, "The first shall be last and the last first" (Matthew 19:30) and "He who humbles himself will be exalted" (Luke 14:11). Yancey explores the subject of suffering at length in numerous of his writings, not least in *Where is God When It Hurts?*[21]

The Bible recounts many times God pays special attention to those who struggle. The Beatitudes (Matthew 5:3–9) are one example. Why would God single out those who suffer for such kind words? Here are five things to learn on the journey through suffering to recovery:

1. **Suffering makes our need for redemption obvious.** This world is imperfect. The need for relief is clear. Suffering shows us our need and promises something better. It helps the believer understand that **a perfect future is in our future** if we pass the test. Peter Marshall, onetime chaplain of the U.S. Senate, said, "God will not permit any troubles to come upon us, unless He has a specific plan by which great blessing can come out of the difficulty."
2. **Jesus Christ is our Redeemer.** He is our only hope for a permanent end to suffering and a perfect future. But we must maintain our faith. Often, He tests us to reveal our true character. Sometimes we pass, sometimes not. A student in a college comparative religions

---
[21] Yancey, Philip, 1977, 1990. Where is God When It Hurts? Zondervan: Grand Rapids

class was deeply hurt by his church. He admitted that he now considered himself a pagan, with an interest in many dark rituals. Only later did it occur to me that **God had put him to the test, and he had failed.** By the way, the same Greek word, πειρασμός-*peirasmos*, is routinely translated as *temptation, trial,* and *testing*.

3. **Redemption is the answer to all our problems.** Only when Jesus Christ restores us from a painful, frustrating, hopeless existence to wholeness does life turn for the better. His renewal alters us mentally and emotionally, physically, spiritually, and socially. It's a *whole–person makeover*.

4. Suffering shows us we are dependent on God and interdependent on each other.

> **BTW**
>
> - **"If you suffer, it must be for sin"** was the human rationale to explain Job's ordeal.
>
> - Still, after God declared Job innocent, the idea of physical punishment for sin persisted. In Jesus's day, the disciples discussed who had sinned, son or parents, to explain the son's blindness. This same belief is common even today.
>
> - Jesus replied that the blindness wasn't because of sin, but in order to display the power of God (John 9).
>
> - **THE LESSON:** *We may never believe that suffering is a good thing. But it's gratifying that often God allows misery in many areas of life in order that His glory might be seen by others.*
>
> - "Lord, give me grace to stand up under whatever trouble You permit. Amen!"

Suffering is intended to drive us into the arms of God. Some, like Charles Templeton, rebel. Others recognize that He wants to turn our temporary anguish and pain into a whole new life of trust, fellowship and productivity. **Love makes God willing to suffer alongside us** in order to heal our pain. Our interdependence on

others can also share the hurt and lift us up when we're too shattered to stand on our own two feet.
5. **Suffering lays bare the difference between wants and needs, luxuries and necessities.** It helps us discover that we can, indeed, live without those things we "can't live without."
6. **Suffering shows us that we're not in control.** God is much better at directing the outcomes of our lives. The sooner we figure that out, the sooner our surrender to Him can begin to restore wholeness to a fragile, fragmented life.

## THE MAN WHO REGAINED IT ALL

**Job gained a new fortune and a new family.** God gave double what Job had before. That's not a promise for everyone. After all, **a lot of suffering IS a natural, logical consequence of our weakness, sins and rebellion.** Job's restoration merely shows God's generosity and the reward for refusing to "curse God and die!"

God also gave Job seven more sons and three daughters. These ten new children didn't "replace" the ten he had lost. But God helped fill that void in Job's heart with more children to comfort him, cheer him, and care for him in his old age.

Solomon's seven hundred wives and three hundred concubines must have produced many children. Seems peculiar that, when writing Psalm 127, the wise king wrote that a man with "a full quiver" of children is blessed.

**Job basked in God's kind words and affirmation.** God rewarded Job for his faithfulness by praising him and telling all those watching the drama that Job was right to defend his own innocence.

God instructed Job to pray for his "friends" who had been so off-target. The Lord accepted Job's intercession for Eliphaz, Bildad, and Zophar. Their "conventional wisdom" was not the reality God used to display Job's godliness for future sufferers! He was blameless and God had a different purpose than simple judgment against sin. **The Lord made the point that suffering could have a redemptive outcome.**

## JOB'S LESSONS FOR YOUR LIFE

**Never forget God's sovereignty.** He rules over Earth and its inhabitants with supreme power and authority. His willingness to impose His universal plan upon creation is seasoned with His love, fairness, and wisdom.

God's supreme knowledge of the entire scope of human endeavor, past, present and future, has been characterized as not just history, but *His story!*

**There's so much we don't know in every painful situation.** This was the error of Job's "friends." They had no idea that God had taken the devil's reins off so that His glory, modeled through Job's righteousness, could be displayed on a global stage. He warned, through Eliphaz, "…man is born to trouble as surely as sparks fly upward." Jesus followed that up in John 16:33 with, **"In this world you will have trouble. But take heart! I have overcome the world."**

It's a comfort, even during troubled times, to know that we may not understand everything, but God does. And He loves us more than we can fathom.

**God is Father and friend, not foe, to the faithful.** An elderly woman in my boyhood church used to say, "When we were out of money, I would remind God, 'Our tithe is paid.'" **Your faithfulness in hard times is worth a ton of gold in eternity.** Being trustworthy, even when you don't see the big picture of what God is thinking, engages His friendship with you. Even as his heart was breaking and his body was screaming with pain, Job stayed true. In turn, God treated him as a trusted friend.

M.R. DeHaan of *Our Daily Bread* tells the story of **a small stick of wood that complained bitterly about its treatment** at the hands of its creator. The craftsman kept whittling away at it, drilling holes in it, filing it down, and sanding it. "It hurts me when you do that," the stick cried out in pain. But the owner kept shaping the wood, drilling a long hole its entire length, ignoring the loud, bitter whining.

Eventually, the plain piece of ebony became a flute which gave great pleasure. Music came from what had been nothing more than firewood. The creator said, "Without these holes and this cutting and shaping, you wouldn't have any complaints, but you would only be a stick. What I'm doing might make you think I'm cruel. Instead, I'm turning you into a beautiful work of art that brings joy to many. Only by cutting you and shaping you painfully, am I able to bring out your greatest value."[22]

So it is with us. God's handiwork sometimes hurts. We suffer or we endure hardship, and we worry that God doesn't care about us. But in fact, **He's turning us into a work of art.** When He's finished, we're able to make beautiful music and bless others' lives.

---

**MOMENT OF TRUTH**

Suffering may seem indiscriminate, but God has a plan for it. He wants your willing cooperation to bless the world through your hardship.

---

**My Personal Journey:** The one lesson from this chapter that speaks loudest to me is:

_____

_____

It says: _____

_____

_____

_____

---

[22] Facebook "Fellowship of the Unashamed" group, February 25, 2016

- Using the internet or *Bartlett's Familiar Quotations*, jot quotations about suffering, especially from a Christian perspective:

_____
_____
_____
_____

- Here is a time God's shaping hurt me, but then resulted in good:

_____
_____
_____
_____

# 7

# A MOTHER'S WORST NIGHTMARE

### JOURNEY TO TRAGEDY AND TRIUMPH
— Mary, Mother of Jesus —
(Luke 1:26–49; 2:19, 34–35; Acts 1:14; 2:1)

Jesse grew up in our small, rural church. She was disadvantaged and faced the future with limited prospects. She gave birth to four children early in life and lived with her husband and kids in a modest house trailer. The dwelling had only a wood stove to fend off the frigid northern winters.

No one knows for sure, but apparently, when stoking the stove during the night, one of the adults left the air draft wide open. Soon, the stove was roaring and belching flames. The house quickly ignited. Jesse and her husband were able to escape the inferno. The children, however, were trapped inside.

The panicked mother ran back into the burning trailer and died with her four children rather than stand outside, wringing her hands as her precious kids lost their lives. Shock and horror gripped the community. Emotions ranged from disbelief to sadness, from grief to outrage, and more.

Today, Jesse is remembered with love only within a small circle of family and friends. Five lives were senselessly snatched away under a winter's frozen glare.

Most mothers' worst nightmares include threats or tragedies of one sort or another involving their children. Even in what some label the "divine family," Mother Mary's worst nightmare came true. It was the humiliating public execution of her innocent firstborn son, Jesus. But thanks to a compassionate Father, tragedies don't always end in crippling shock and cyclical nightmares.

His was no ordinary life, nor death, and the far-reaching results of Jesus's life, death, and resurrection are the fulcrum of God's plan to rescue us from sin and offer eternal life. In time, Mary herself would see the godly, eternal outcome of her own worst nightmare. It was a journey to tragedy and onward, to triumph, the likes of which no one could have foretold. Oh, wait! The prophets did exactly that!

## MARY WAS, BY ALL EXISTING ACCOUNTS, A WONDERFUL PERSON

**She led a godly girlhood and was highly favored by Yahweh God.** The world's most famous mother has been elevated to uber-saint status, even divinity, by some. The Immaculate Conception is the doctrine that Mary was without a sin nature from the moment she was conceived by her parents. But according to the Bible, she was not sinless. If she had been, why not have *her* die to take our punishment for sin?

Jesus was the only human without original sin. Romans 3:23 sets the standard: no one measures up to God's glory. Jesus Christ, God the Son, is history's only exception to the otherwise universal human status of "sinner."

Mary was a fine girl who led a godly life. She probably impressed those who knew her well. She was taken aback by the angel's words,

"Greetings, you who are highly favored. The Lord is with you." The angel reassured her, "Do not be afraid, Mary; you have found favor with God."

Jesus's mother-to-be was a girl anyone would love to have as a daughter. She was a credit to her family and a citizen of which Nazareth must have been proud—until the scandalous pregnancy, that is.

**The divine Holy Spirit entered the human realm through Mary's virgin womb.** The girl (traditions say she may have been as young as twelve to fourteen years old) was understandably confused. "How can I be this baby's mother since I am a virgin?" she asked in puzzlement. The angel of God explained, "The Holy Spirit will come on you...so the holy one to be born will be called the Son of God."

Caught up in the joy of this revelation, Mary exclaimed, "My soul glorifies the Lord and my spirit rejoices in God my Savior...From now on all generations will call me blessed, for the Mighty One has done great things for me—holy is his name" (Luke 1:46–49).

**Mary knew from the beginning that Jesus was special, as no other child had ever been nor would be again.** He was God the Savior, come in the flesh, piercing the darkness with heavenly light. The angel's words identified the boy to be born as the special, one-of-a-kind Messiah who would bring peace to His entire creation.

> God loves to do extraordinary things through ordinary people, empowered by His strength.

Every girl in Israel hoped to be the mother of the Chosen One of God. There were certainly disagreements about His role. Would He be a military conqueror? Would He bring Rome to the negotiating table and hammer out political independence for Israel? Certainly He would incorporate a spiritual dimension, but how would that interface with His expected military-political leadership? What was it that would make Him so special?

Most translations of John 3:16 identify Jesus as the "only begotten" Son of God. When "only begotten" is dissected in the original text, however, a case can be made for translating it as **"the special, one–of–a–kind" Son.** The New Testament language uses a compound word here, μονο–γενη, [mono– (*one*) and –genê (*type* or *kind*)]. Everyone who trusts Jesus as Savior is a daughter or son of God (John 1:12). Jesus, however, is the special, one–of–a–kind Son of God, unlike any other, before or since. He is the divine God the Son.

And now Mary knew that, on her miraculous journey, God had chosen her to bear this highly–anticipated, special, unique kind of child who would grow up to save the world from itself.

## MARY WAS THE MATRIX

A 'matrix' constitutes the place from which something else originates.[23] For example, the harsh, unjust reparations forced on Germany after World War–I were the matrix from which the deadly World War–II sprang forth.

**It was society's nature that raised the red flag.** Sometimes, a member of society who is viewed in a favorable light makes decisions and acts in ways that suddenly cast them in a negative light. Electric carmaker Elon Musk was a darling of the climate change media. Then he came out in favor of free speech! Suddenly the red flags were flapping in the breeze.

Mary's unexplained pregnancy caused ostracism. A society like first–century Israel would never accept an out–of–wedlock pregnancy. Social–religious norms would not allow it. The previously darling of the town was now anathema!

***Shunning* was the first level of rejection.** Both Joseph and Mary knew they had not caved to sexual passion. But everyone else would assume either that they were partners in this unexpected pregnancy or that Mary had cheated on Joseph. And so she was excluded from polite society.

---

[23] www.dictionary.com

Jewish law permitted divorce for an engaged couple, either quietly or with the din of public denunciation. In the Old Testament, Mary's supposed dalliance would've been enough for stoning. Joseph's inclination was a quiet, don't-rock-the-boat divorce. He loved her enough that he was reluctant to shame her.

Two thousand years later, we understand that there was no moral downfall. Mary was pregnant by the agency of God the Holy Spirit. Both she and Joseph were blameless. But there was probably a murky stigma attached to her name. Today, she is mother extraordinaire for all Christendom.

**Mary contributed to God the Son's human character.** How could a godly, principled matron of her caliber be anything other than a wonderful influence on her child? As we know today, Jesus was the 100-percent divine God the Son. He was also the 100-percent human son of Mary. This second aspect of the Savior was nurtured and crafted by His mother and others, including Joseph, we may assume. He learned integrity, ethics, compassion, and many other altruistic qualities that contributed to His sterling human makeup. Mary was His matrix into humanity.

God found the matriarchal traits He required for His Son's earthly birth and upbringing in Mary, a humble, pure girl in a backward Jewish town hidden in the Galilean outback. He chose Nazareth, not the London, Paris, or New York of that day. This was the girl God wanted to birth and cherish the one-of-a-kind divine and human Son of God.

## DID JESUS USE HIS DIVINE NATURE ON EARTH?

This dual divine-human nature of Jesus raises a question, debated for two millennia. How could He be both fully God and fully human? **Was He the "200-percent man?"** Whose 'rithmetic would allow for such a contradiction? God's divine math supersedes ours in this critically important dimension.

Philippians 2:5–11 reveals that all of His miracles of nature, resurrecting dead people, multiplying fish and bread, controlling nature, and speaking with authority for God the Father, were accomplished without using His own divine powers. Above all, His own resurrection, after three days in the tomb, was accomplished not by His position as God the Son, but as a result of His faith in God the Father and the Holy Spirit.[24]

Paul explained this truth in what is known today as the "Kenotic" passage (Philippians 2:7), Greek for "He emptied Himself." He asserted that Jesus voluntarily gave up His divine powers in order to become human and redeem fallen humanity ("rather, [Jesus] made himself nothing by taking the very nature of a servant, being made in human likeness"). Jesus did signs and wonders the same way Team Jesus would in the ensuing two millennia, by prayer and abiding in Christ, yielding to the Holy Spirit, and exercising obedient faith in God.

Numerous Bible passages offer proof of this, and one verse nails it: "And if the Spirit of him who raised Jesus from the dead is living in you, he who raised Christ from the dead will also give life to your mortal bodies because of his Spirit who lives in you" (Romans 8:11).

## MARY WAS ON TEAM JESUS

I forgot what T–shirt I was wearing one Spring day when I walked out of Walmart. Three teenage girls were heading inside, and one girl shouted at me, "Hey, we're teammates!" Startled, I quickly put two and three together. My shirt said, **"Team Jesus."** I gave her a thumbs up. Millions have joined Team Jesus in these past two thousand years, but none more passionately, I suspect, than His mother.

**Mary heard and saw many thought–provoking events.** Dedicating the eight–day–old Jesus at the temple, she pondered the words of righteous Simeon. "Sovereign Lord," he prayed, holding the infant Jesus

---

[24] Examine this subject at Did Jesus cease to be God on Earth? | www.evidenceunseen.com

in his arms, "my eyes have seen your salvation...a light for revelation to the Gentiles, and the glory of your people Israel."

Then, Simeon turned to the new mother and prophesied, "This child is destined to cause the falling and rising of many in Israel... And a sword will pierce your own soul, too." It was a hint at the tragedy (and triumph) to come.

Soon, the prophetess Anna spoke up. She "gave thanks to God and spoke about the child to all who were looking forward to the redemption of Jerusalem" (Luke 2:25-38).

Finding Jesus at the temple when, as a twelve-year-old savant, He was schooling the religious experts, Mary and Joseph were confused. Why would the lad ask, "Didn't you know that I must be in my Father's house?" His father's house was in Nazareth, wasn't it?

After this, Luke writes, "his mother treasured all these things in her heart. And Jesus grew in *wisdom* and *stature*, and in *favor with God* and *man*" (*italics* added). Luke 2:52 is evidence that we humans,

> **BTW**
>
> - **Six Marys.** At least six women named 'Mary' are identified in the New Testament.
>
> - Mary, Lazarus's and Martha's sister. We know the most about this Mary, who was once a harlot who poured perfume on Jesus's feet. Her desire to sit and learn from Jesus shows she was a redeemed person.
>
> - Mary Magdalene was freed of seven demons. Many speculate she was the woman caught in adultery (John 7:53–8:12), though the Bible doesn't confirm that.
>
> - Another Mary was the mother of James the Younger, Joseph and Salome (Mark 15:40); note that Jesus had half-brothers who bore those names also).
>
> - Apostles James and John had a mother named Mary, wife of Zebedee.
>
> - Mary, the wife of Clopas, stood at the foot of the cross when Jesus was crucified.
>
> - Mary, the mother of Jesus, saw His crucifixion, later prayed with the believers, and perhaps saw Jesus ascend to His Heavenly Father.

created in God's image, function within four primary realms: He grew in wisdom (mental, emotional realm) and in stature (physical). He grew in favor with God (spiritual realm) and with man (social).

Jesus's first miracle at the wedding in Cana also caused Mary to ponder Team Jesus. She had an inkling of His power when she told Jesus that the wine was all gone. His reply, "Woman, why do you involve Me?" reveals a gentle rebuke for His beloved mother (much like a shy child hiding behind his mother's skirt, resisting her gentle push to the center of attention).

Mary saw the horror while standing at the foot of the cross. After church one Sunday morning, I chatted with congregation members on the porch of our Ohio church. Suddenly, a screech of brakes snapped my head toward the street. With cries of alarm, we watched as Daniel Rodriguez darted into the street toward his home across the way. I wanted to spin away, to spare myself the violent death of an innocent child. But I could not. I was frozen by the impending tragedy. Thankfully, the driver saw the toddler and was able to stop in time (hence, the shriek of tires on the pavement).

John 19:26–27 confirms that, horror and grief aside, **Jesus's mother was an eyewitness to His horrible murder.** Like a time when you're unable to tear your eyes away from a tragedy, Mary wanted to be anywhere else. But her mother–love kept her riveted to the spot as the unspeakable nightmare unfolded before her eyes.

Standing at the cross, overwhelmed by all the terrible events of the day, Mary's downward journey to tragedy hit rock bottom. But soon it would climb to triumphant new heights of hope and joy.

**Did Mary see Jesus alive after the resurrection?** The Bible doesn't specifically say, but how could she not? He remained on earth for forty days after rising from the dead. Hundreds of people at one time and place saw Him, according to Paul (1 Corinthians 15:6). He traveled the length and breadth of Israel, being seen by and ministering to many individuals at other times. It's tempting to speculate that Mary saw her firstborn son, too. Could all this have happened without Jesus encountering His mother? They were very likely together more than once, perhaps often!

There is confusion about Mother Mary's activities immediately following the crucifixion, partly because there were at least six *Mary*s mentioned in the Gospels.

**Mary was possibly at the Ascension.** Acts 1:6–14 offers a glimpse of Jesus's life between resurrection and return to the Father. It seems likely that Mother Mary was closely involved with this last month–plus of His human activities.

He had made it clear to His followers that He was soon returning to His Father. Most mothers would spend as much time as possible with a son who was soon departing.[25]

**Mary was praying in the Upper Room with the others.** Acts 1:14 says the disciples were constantly praying, along with "the women and Mary the mother of Jesus, and with his brothers." She likely wielded Team Jesus influence with His once–skeptical half–brothers James, Jude, Joseph, and Simon. The first two eventually wrote New Testament books.

Team Jesus was obedient to the Lord's command to wait for the outpouring of the Holy Spirit, as reported in Acts chapter 2.

We don't know Mary's role or activities after her Son ascended. But she was a player on Team Jesus. That fact gave meaning and purpose to this lifelong journey she had traveled, through tragedy to triumph. An Orthodox legend purports that Mary died in AD 48. It's not important because the Bible leaves Mary's life silent beyond Acts 1:14. Any guesses beyond that are simply conjecture.

**Mary had a Holy Spirit experience.** All the way back at the annunciation (Luke chapter 1), archangel Gabriel informed Mary that "The

---

[25] Notice the detailed explanation of this in the sidebar "BTW," p. 69

Holy Spirit will come on you, and the power of the Most High will overshadow you..."

Mary was equipped with God-given spiritual gifts to be used for ministry, as are all believers. The rest of her life was set aside (sanctified) for God's sacred use. It's antithetical to assume that her usefulness ended when Jesus returned to heaven.

**The Phoenix is a mythical bird from Greek mythology.** It dies, only to rise again from the ashes of its destruction. It provides a metaphor illustrating the truth that dead or dying dreams need not stay as they are; you can experience a rebirth of hope. Phoenix is a myth, but hope is a reality for believers.

Christians see Jesus's death and resurrection not as a product of storytellers, but a real-life event filled with the hope Christ offers, even in the midst of tragedy. Only He can give "...a crown of beauty instead of ashes, the oil of joy instead of mourning and a garment of praise instead of a spirit of despair." (Isaiah 61:3). He's eager to renew courage and purpose in the life of anyone whose trust is founded in Him.

---

**MOMENT OF TRUTH**

The anguish of your worst nightmare can be assuaged as God redeems your life and brings beauty from the ashes.

---

**MY PERSONAL JOURNEY:** Here is a time in my life when tragedy resulted in triumph:

_____
_____
_____
_____

- Let me describe the matrix from which my faith has emerged:

  _____
  _____
  _____
  _____
  _____

- With God's strength and love I will work to turn tragedy into an opportunity for good in life. ☐ Yes ☐ No
- I will look for people suffering tragic circumstances and try to help them in this way:

  _____
  _____
  _____
  _____
  _____

**Grasp the truths of this lesson in YouTube: Shadow of a Tree – Christine Wyrtzen**

# 8

# SLIP OUT THE BACK, JACK

**JOURNEY OUT OF DEPRESSION**
— Elijah —
(1 Kings 18:16–46; 19:1–18)

Walking through the narrow, serpentine streets of Hong Kong, New York Pastor and author, Norman Vincent Peale, came upon a tattoo studio. In the window were displayed samples of the artwork available. You could have an anchor, flag, mermaid or whatever you wanted, hot–inked somewhere on your body. Doctor Peale was struck with force by three words that could be tattooed on your flesh: "Born to Lose."

"I entered the shop in astonishment," Peale recalled. Pointing to those words, he asked the tattoo artist, "Does anyone really have that terrible phrase, 'Born to lose,' tattooed on his body?" He replied, "Yes, sometimes." Peale said, "But, I just can't believe that anyone in his right mind would do that." The tattooer simply tapped his forehead and said, "Before tattoo on body, tattoo on mind."[26]

## ELIJAH'S WEAKNESS AND GOD'S POWER

**Experience God's power on a journey to strength.** God told Elijah

---

[26] Norman Vincent Peale, The Power of the Plus Factor. New York: Fawcett Pub-lications, 1988.

to challenge the priests of Baal to prove which one was really God. When he asked the people whom they favored, they were predictably non-committal. They would follow whoever came out on top.

The priests of Baal howled, cried, chanted, ranted and cut themselves to bloody ribbons. No response!

Elijah even taunted them to a heightened frenzy. Maybe Baal is deep in thought, he proposed. Shout louder! Maybe Baal is busy with something else. The original Hebrew in this verse (1 Kings 18:27) suggests, **"Maybe he is on the toilet!"** Shout louder! Maybe Baal has gone off on a trip and cannot hear you. Shout louder! Finally, near sunset, the priests of Baal could not continue.

Elijah built an altar, soaked the sacrifice with water, and asked God just once, quietly, to display His power. God sent fire from heaven and consumed sacrifice, altar, soil and water. Finally, the people were willing to take sides. Who would not agree that such a powerful God

## BTW

- **ELIJAH** is one of only two people in the Bible who did not die.
- Genesis 5:24 says God "took Enoch away," apparently because of his godliness.
- The prophet Elijah also departed earth without dying. In 2 Kings 2:11 he was taken up from earth by a fiery chariot, as his successor, Elisha watched.
- One notable event in Elijah's life is the account of his feeding by the ravens (1 Kings 17).
- After informing King Ahab that a deadly famine was coming, God sent Elijah east of the Jordan River to protect him. He drank from a brook and God sent birds to deliver food.
- God performed many miracles through Elijah, including raising a lad to life again.
- **THE LESSON:** *God plus one person is always a majority. And He is looking for a few good men and women to accomplish His global plan.*

is truly the One? But things were not so good when they all arrived at Samaria, the capital city of Israel's ten northern tribes.

**Forgetting God's power is a journey to depression.** Queen Jezebel was the real power behind Israel's Baal cult, and she was not a happy camper. After Elijah executed four hundred priests of Baal on Mt. Carmel, Jezebel issued orders that Elijah must die for his crime of proving that Baal was powerless.

What could Elijah's responses have been to the royal threat? He might have said, "I'll die when *God* says I will die, and not a moment before!" Or, "You and whose army will kill me?" He might have jeered, "Jezebel, you are powerless before God." Even a threat might have been used, "You wanna see fireworks? I'll show you fireworks! Start running!"

Instead, Elijah, the prophet of the most potent force on the planet, "ran for his life." This journey was not one of courage, but cowardice. His headlong flight occurred simultaneously with his burgeoning depression. He sat under a tree in the middle of nowhere and prayed that he might die. God didn't argue or even reason with Elijah. Instead, He let him sleep. Then, God fed and strengthened him physically. The body can contribute greatly to depression, medical researchers say. Rested and nourished, Elijah traveled forty days without food and drink to Mount Sinai. This was where Moses received the Ten Commandments.

**Rediscovering God's power is a journey to recovery.** Elijah found a cave and went inside to spend the night. Two separate times God asked, "What are you doing here, Elijah?" Both times Elijah offered a puny human rationalization. Both times he gave the same explanation, "I'm the only one left who honors You, God. And now they're trying to kill me."

Between these two identical conversations, God displayed His awesome power. He sent a wind so strong that it shattered rock! But alas, Elijah didn't find God in the wind.

> **A carnal paradox: Depression can come from being self-centered and thinking only of yourself.**

Next, there was an earthquake, but Elijah didn't discover God in that, either. Then, a raging wildfire broke out, but God was nowhere in the flames. Finally, Elijah heard God in a still, small voice.

We often look for God in the roar, the spectacle, the amazing displays of power. But usually, God wants us to listen for His quiet words. Until we tune out the noise and clamor, and tune in the soft, gentle whisper of God, we'll continue to scuffle with depression.

**Exercising God's power is a journey to achievement.** God clearly understood that Elijah needed to refocus outside himself and his problems. He was telling Elijah, "I'm not finished with you. I still have important things for you to do." Elijah obeyed; he went and did those things God assigned to him. There is no more sign of depression in the biblical record.

God indicated to Elijah that he was still part of His great plan for the world. Elijah realized that his work—and his life—were not over.

When God assured him that there were still seven thousand others who had not turned away to idols, Elijah was encouraged. He continued to be a productive component of God's plan. One day, God took him up to heaven in a chariot of fire.

## SEEDS OF DEPRESSION

**Never forget God's power.** Like Elijah, it's very easy, in the chaos of life, to overlook God's might. When you see so much evil around you, it can be hard to remember how God has used His power to bless the world. When you forget that God is above all else and that you have a vital role in His plan, falling into depression is easier than falling off a log.

**Don't let your problems overwhelm you.** Like Elijah, the problems in our everyday lives can overwhelm us. Maybe you've had the very same thought he had. "I'm the only believer left. I'm all alone out here." Loneliness is discouraging. Elijah felt isolated from other people of faith. That isolation sent him spiraling downward into despair. Vern McLellan says,

**"Discouragement is faith in the devil."**

Maybe it feels like you're fighting a losing battle. You try to do what's right, but there are so many influences against righteousness, it seems hopeless. Remember, Elijah's depression came on the heels of a great victory. God showed His power in an amazing way. Immediately following that, Elijah's life is threatened—what a crushing letdown!

**Don't feed the "poor little me" animal.** As all these seeds of depression grow, our focus turns inward more and more. Soon you're wallowing in self-pity! The whole world seems against you. "I can't catch a break, no matter what I do. I do what's right and look what happens. So-and-so is out to get me. Poor little me!"

**Don't apply the human "fix."** In the crucible of depression, Elijah, the man of God, did what human nature often does. He thought of a human way to fix the painful situation. He prayed that he might die (19:4). The human fix is usually just a response to the falsehoods of the Great Liar, Satan. Proverbs 14:12 says it so concisely: **"There is a way that seems right to a man, but in the end, it leads to death."**

The sinful nature's default setting is to look for human solutions, but often they are destructive. They're not at all the way God wants to fix a situation. "For My thoughts are not your thoughts, neither are My ways the ones you would take," the Lord explains. "In the same way that the heavens are higher than the earth, so My ways are higher than yours, and My thoughts than yours. (Isaiah 55:8, 9).

Such impotent human reasoning is common in the history of this country. In 1863, Abraham Lincoln called for a national day of fasting and prayer. In the throes of wartime agony, the President said, "We have forgotten the gracious Hand which has preserved us in peace and multiplied and enriched and strengthened us. We have vainly imagined in the deceitfulness of our hearts that all these blessings were produced by some superior wisdom and virtue of our own."

The human 'fix' for life's problems disregards God's quiet voice of comfort, love and guidance. If we're willing to find and follow God's solution to our situation, He will turn frustration, sadness, despair and depression into victory.

## TRIUMPH OVER DEPRESSION

**Remember God's power.** Turn your thoughts to God's mighty ways in your past and present. Retell some of the great things He has done, both in the Bible and in everyday life. When you remember that all-powerful God is in control, you'll be able to believe that He will make things turn out for the best in your life too.

It's not enough to remember and retell God's great victories in the Bible. Embrace the wonderful things God has done in this temporal life, the here-and-now. If God is only powerful in history, then perhaps He's not God of the present and future. Read books about what He has done in the near past.

**Embrace God's assignments.** Review some of the projects God has assigned you in the past—ways He has put your skills and interests to work for His Kingdom. Elijah could've avoided great personal turmoil if he had just recalled to mind the contest against Baal.

Next, make sure you are exactly where God wants you, in the present. That endeavor might demand some changes. God will reveal them to you and help you change to become what He envisioned for you when you were created.

Ask God to show you what He wants you to do in the future. It's a great encouragement, knowing that God has an important plan for your life. Knowing that you can choose to live out that plan, life is not over.

With God's divine help and wisdom, you'll come to believe that the best days of God's life for you may still be ahead. He's just getting you warmed up for the really great things He's still planning for you.

**Hold onto God's encouragement.** God encouraged Elijah by advising him, "Yet I reserve seven thousand in Israel—all whose knees have not bowed down to Baal. You may feel alone, but you're not. My resources are undiminished by the evil all around you."

God reassures you today, "You are not alone. I am with you." He promises that the Body of Christ—fellow believers—can encourage and support you in times of depression. By human standards, life may look hopeless. But not to God. He breathes hope into those who will trust Him to keep His promises of love, strength and purpose. **Rest assured—God's not finished with you yet**.

You may not feel that God still wants to use you. You may not feel you're worth His effort. But don't let human reasoning muffle God's voice. He loves you and wants to bless your life beyond imagination.

**Mundane assignments can show promise.** A tutor assigned to help children in a city hospital received a routine request that she visit a particular child. She took the boy's name and room number and was told by his teacher, "We're studying nouns and adverbs in his class now. Please help him with his homework so he doesn't fall behind the others."

Not until the visiting teacher arrived at the boy's hospital room did she realize it was in the burn unit. No one had prepared her to find a young boy horribly burned and in great suffering. She couldn't just turn and walk out, so she awkwardly stammered, "I am the hospital tutor. Your school teacher sent me to help you with nouns and adverbs."

The next morning a nurse in the burn unit intercepted her. "What did you do to that boy?" Before the teacher could start a profusion of apologies, the nurse interrupted. "You don't understand. We've been very worried about him, but ever since you were here yesterday, his whole attitude has changed. He's fighting back, responding to treatment. It's as though he has decided to live."

The boy later explained that he had completely given up hope until he saw that teacher. It all changed when he came to a simple conclusion. With joyful tears he explained, **"They wouldn't send a teacher to work on nouns and adverbs with a dying boy, would they?"**

On anyone's journey through life, encouragement is powerful medicine. Be hopeful if you have struggled with depression. God's not finished with you yet.

> **MOMENT OF TRUTH**
>
> Forgetting God and fixating on self can lead to serious depression. When you rediscover His power and listen for His voice, He can heal you and do powerful, exciting things for and through you.

**My Personal Journey:** I have experienced God's power, but then have forgotten it. Here's what can help me rediscover it:

_____
_____
_____
_____

- I could do this to break the isolation that often accompanies depression:

_____
_____
_____
_____

- Here's how I have tried to apply the human "fix?" What was the result?

_____
_____
_____

- Here's how I can use God's *power*, *assignments* and *reassurance* to refocus outside of myself and my own problems:

# 9

# WALK ON THE WILD SIDE

**JOURNEY THROUGH RISK TO REWARD**
— Esther —
(Esther 1–10)

**Embark on a "wild side" journey.** The quintessential wild side daredevil stunt happened at Niagara Falls in 1859. A French tightrope walker, Blondin, balanced his way across the gorge on a specially made rope three inches thick and 1,100 feet long. Another time he toted a small stove and cooked an omelet halfway across.[27]

Tightrope walking remained popular, but showoffs were already cooking up new ideas to dazzle the spectators. English immigrant Carlisle Graham rode a barrel over the falls in 1886. Many more followed suit, with activity rising to a peak in 1901.

A plump 63-year-old schoolteacher took things to the next level. Annie Taylor packed an oak barrel with a lucky heart-shaped pillow, a mattress, and an anvil for ballast and took the plunge over Niagara Falls. She was fished out below, seventy-five minutes after she went over, bruised and shaken, but alive. She told onlookers, "No one ought ever do that again."

---

[27] cf. Daredevils of Niagara Falls (niagarafallslive.com) www.niagrafalls live.com/ daredevils_of_niagara, for more on this subject

"Evel" Knievel traversed the wild side on motorcycles. He was best known for the Snake River jump in 1974, when the parachute on his rocket bike accidentally deployed upon launch. It dragged him down into the canyon, where he almost drowned.[28] During his career, Evel broke thirty-five bones in his body, the most ever, according to the *Guinness Book of World Records*.

The "Crocodile Hunter," Australia's Steve Irwin, wrestled crocs, handled many dangerous animals, and generally lived on the wild side. He died in 2006 after being stung by a stingray through the heart.[29]

One Bible woman made a different sort of "Walk on the Wild Side." She took a short, yet critically important, journey into forbidden territory.

## CLEAR AND PRESENT DANGER

**Esther seized her *carpe diem* opportunity.** Vashti, the reigning Queen of Persia, committed insubordination and was deposed by King Xerxes. Subsequently, Xerxes conducted a year-long search for a new queen. He filled his harem with the most beautiful women of his empire. The Bible doesn't say anything about the morality of this. Esther was selected for her beauty, intelligence and poise. Without this opportunity, the means to save her people might never have materialized.

**Mordecai lived by his integrity.** Meanwhile, Esther's cousin, Mordecai, a gatekeeper for the King, overheard a plot to assassinate Xerxes. Mordecai could easily have ignored the threat. What was it to him if the king of Persia, Israel's oppressor, was assassinated? Yet, true to his integrity, Mordecai reported the conspiracy and the scheme was thwarted.

**Haman made an existential threat.** Xerxes's Prime Minister was Haman, a pathological anti-Semite. He fomented a plan to kill all the

---

[28] cf. Evel Knievel's Famous Snake River Canyon Jump Smithsonian Magazine www.smithsonianmag.com/videos/evel-knievels-famous-snake-river-canyon-jump
[29] Steve Irwin | Biography, Death, Son, Daughter, Wife, & Facts | Britannica • www.britannica.com/biography/Steve-Irwin

Jews of Persia. Somehow, he sold the idea to the King. Neither man knew that the Queen was an expatriate Jew.

When Haman announced to the public his plot to exterminate the Jews, Mordecai got word to Esther, the cousin he had raised. She did not know because she was sequestered in the palace. His message sent a chill up her spine. "Don't think that because you're in the king's household, you alone of all the Jews will survive," he warned her. "If you remain silent at this time, relief and deliverance for the Jews will arise from another quarter. But you and your father's family will die. And who knows, perhaps you have become Queen for such a time as this?" (Esther 4:13–16).

Mordecai implied that God would save His people through some other means if Queen Esther chose to avoid the risk. It seemed obvious that Esther was in this position of influence by God's hand. She had a responsibility to save her people.

Mordecai's principle was, "God is not limited by your relative willingness to act!" God elevated Esther for this purpose, but if she refused to cooperate, God was not stymied in His effort to save the Jews. He could employ other strategies if He chose.

**Esther developed a plan.** The obvious solution was for the Jewish Queen to ask her King for help. But how could she let him know that Haman's treachery endangered her personally? She must walk, unannounced and uninvited, into the throne room. Persian law said she could be executed for doing so without authorization. Ironically, it was the opposite problem Queen Vashti had. She refused to go to Xerxes when summoned.

If Esther had refused to help, she would have been the loser, not God and not the Jewish people. It's always unwise to believe that God is out of options. If you think you're God's last, best hope, think again.

## PERSONAL RISK, CORPORATE REWARD

**"If I die, I die!"** Esther recognized that preserving her own life was not the most important thing in this crisis. Many people never make this discovery. Saving their own skin is paramount. Esther readily accepted the fact that her life was only one piece of a much larger puzzle. Soldiers who do heroic things in battle often have made this discovery. "If I live while many others die, could I live with myself? Would I even want to?"

More than four hundred years after Esther said, "If I die, I die!" Jesus said, "Whoever tries to keep their life will lose it, and whoever loses their life will preserve it" (Luke 17:33).

Esther must have been thinking that even if she were executed for going into the king's presence uninvited, she would be no more dead than being killed in Haman's plot just because she was Jewish. She also demonstrated a godly attitude. If her death would somehow save her people, it would be a fair exchange. This was precisely Jesus's attitude on the cross (Philippians 2:5–11).

## HEROIC RESULT

> Lucy was anxious about meeting Aslan. "Is he quite safe? I shall feel rather nervous about meeting a lion..." "Safe?" said Mr. Beaver ... "Of course he isn't safe. But He's good. He's the King..."
> – C.S. Lewis, *The Lion, the Witch and the Wardrobe*

**The evil plot is revealed.** After dressing for the occasion, Esther made the short journey and stood outside Xerxes's throne room. This was "the moment of truth." Esther's attempt to save her people would succeed or fail at this critical intersection.

When the King saw his Queen waiting to enter, he was pleased and held out his royal scepter, granting her permission to approach. With a sigh of relief, she invited the King and his Prime Minister—that wicked Haman—to a private luncheon.

With only Haman and Xerxes in attendance, Esther explained how the Jewish extermination scheme, hatched by Haman and approved by the King, would cost her life, and the King his Queen.

**The wicked plot is foiled.** From this point on, the story picked up speed as it rolled downhill. Esther carried forward the plan to save the Jews. The King realized what had happened, and so did Haman.

His plot to destroy the Jews failed because God intended to save them. Esther played her brief but vital part. God used her willingness, even to die if necessary, to save His people, the Jews.

**The deadly plot is reversed.** Not only were the Jewish people rescued, the plotter was stripped bare, exposed for the sinister hater he was. Because of Esther's willingness to get involved, to take the risk, Haman paid the ultimate price for his wickedness. His downfall is a lesson to many. You cannot win when you fight against God.

## OUR JOURNEY OF RISK AND REWARD

**"Risk the danger, reap the reward."** What's at risk when you consider a wild, frightening journey? It might be your prosperity, reputation or safety. And don't forget today's ubiquitous demands from cancel culture. Then there's popularity, personal happiness and the all-important success endangered by rocking the boat. It may be all these things, but there's usually more.

What's truly at risk is more crucial. It's a matter of who you really are. It's a question of personal courage and the defense of your convictions. At its root, it's **right living according to God's word.** The real question is, "Are you that kind of person?"

Sometimes that cannot be known until you're under the gun, dodging life's burning bullets. Under a burden, facing major risks, what will you do? Will your actions, when facing the withering fire of battle, reveal the person you really are? Will you be who God wants you to be, do what God wants you to do? This is a crucial consideration.

The words of Jesus teach this principle. "Whoever wants to be my disciple must deny themselves, take up their cross and follow me...What good is it for someone to gain the whole world yet forfeit their soul? What can anyone give in exchange for their soul?" (Mark 8:34, 36–37).

This simple yet powerful Bible lesson teaches that spiritual matters are infinitely more important than matters of the physical realm! Take the risk. Follow God's plan, whatever it is. Discount issues of the present; reap eternal rewards.

Moses believed disgrace for the sake of Christ was of greater value than the temporary treasures of Egypt. He was looking ahead to his eternal reward (Hebrews 11:24) and cast lesser things aside.

In Stephen Covey's book *First Things First*, there's a comparison of the clock and the compass. He observes that many people run their lives by the *clock*. Every decision is made according to a temporal rhythm. Not very inspiring or meaningful, but certainly well-ordered. In this economy, life is measured by how many things get done.

Instead, says Covey, try organizing life using a *compass*. Where are you headed? What is your life's direction? Are you on course to accomplish vital things? Have you traveled a meaningful path? What values do your decisions reveal? What's the quality of your work?

Avoid putting your personal interests ahead of the common good, especially when the project is life-changing. Act like Esther! Making a major, life-altering journey when the stakes are high—now *that* is Walking on the Wild Side.

---

### MOMENT OF TRUTH

Life sometimes demands great courage, as you're called to Journey through danger to bless and enrich the lives of others. God promises to make that journey with us.

---

**MY PERSONAL JOURNEY:** I can see myself making the decision Esther made, to risk her own life to save her people. ❒ Yes ❒ I'm thinking ❒ No way

- I may never be called on to do something noble and heroic, but I'm willing, God, if You'll go with me. ❒ Yes ❒ No
- The following scale indicates my current attitude:

| −5 −4 −3 −2 −1 | 0 +1 +2 | +3 +4 +5 |
|---|---|---|
| My own welfare first | I am clearly conflicted | Others before me |

- This is a journey I may never need to make. But with God's help, I'll be faithful in putting others' needs high on my priority list in this way:

_____
_____
_____
_____
_____

# 10

# LIKE A GOOD NEIGHBOR

**JOURNEY TO SERVE THE NEEDY**
— The Good Samaritan —
(Luke 10:25–37)

The *Gainesville* (FL) *Sun* newspaper reported a neighborly kindness in which Shaquille O'Neal, retired basketball superstar, played a part. He stands seven-feet, one-inch tall and weighs 325 pounds, after all, so he is truly larger than life.

Cindy Swirko of the *Sun* reported: Recently, an unnamed woman crashed her car when her tire blew out on I-75. When police arrived, she was not alone. The dash cam showed a seven-foot-tall Good Samaritan.

Shaq was driving behind the vehicle when the accident occurred. When he witnessed the crash, he didn't simply call 911—he didn't leave it to someone else. He pulled over and got personally involved.

One of the kids from the damaged car was actually hanging out with the sports legend, near Shaq's car, when police arrived. O'Neal fist-bumped a deputy and walked back to the damaged car with the officers to tell the family goodbye. Once assistance arrived, he got in his vehicle and left. He didn't stay around for the photo op. He was just a concerned citizen, a neighbor, a Good Samaritan who walked a mile in someone else's shoes (Shaq's own shoes are size 22).[30]

## JESUS ACED THE TEST

**A lawyer hit Jesus with a legal puzzler.** He was often tested this way, as enemies looked to entrap Him in His words and prove Him a bumbling dunce or worse. Imagine the snickering between Pharisees as the trap was laid. They had seen it before. In fact, some of them had probably tried it before. So their sniggering was partly, "Let's see Jesus wiggle out of this one." It may also have been, "Good luck trying to trap this guy into embarrassing (or even blasphemous) statements to be used against him in a court of law." According to the New Testament record, Jesus was always up to the task of defending the truth. Not once did they succeed in trapping Him with His responses. So, the lawyer asked, "What must I do to inherit eternal life?"

What's with this "inherit eternal life" idea? Someone has observed that God has no grandchildren. Eternal life is not a part of anyone's spiritual last will and testament. You simply **cannot inherit eternal life**. You can only accept God's gift of grace and use it for all it's worth. I'm surprised Jesus didn't take this opportunity to point that out. But He had bigger fish to fry at the moment. Outside this context, the Bible makes it perfectly clear that **eternal life is never earned nor inherited**; it's only given by a gracious, generous God.

**Jesus turned the tables.** So the "inherit eternal life" question was hanging out there. As usual, Jesus knew how to deal with it. He turned the tables and put the lawyer on the spot instead. "What does Moses's law say about your question?" He asked. "How do you read it?" A great way to turn the tables is to ask a questioner their opinion. If the questioner is familiar with the Bible, ask what the Bible says. As soon as the

---

[30] See the video from FL State Patrol dashcam at: Shaq stops to help stranded Flori-da driver - YouTube • www.youtube.com/watch?v=DRERpMIj6KY

words left Jesus's mouth, the legal expert found himself back on his heels. The questioner became the questioned; the hunter became the hunted.

**Turned tables can make great serving surfaces.** The objective is not simply to win the argument. The purpose of engaging in biblical discussion is to find ways to meet needs, so that lives can be changed for God.

Turning tables is one of Jesus's primary methods to confront us with the need for radical change. With no other avenue of escape, the lawyer admitted that the Jewish law instructed the reader to "'Love the Lord your God with all your heart and with all your soul and with all your strength and with all your mind' (Deuteronomy 6:5) and, 'Love your neighbor as yourself.'"

"Do this and you will live" Jesus replied, making the point that it's not enough to know the right answer. It only matters when you turn knowledge into action. **"Apply or die" is an appropriate adage for any biblical truth.** It zeros

### BTW

- **Verbal Traps.** There are numerous examples in the New Testament of skeptics (mostly experts in the religious law) trying to catch Jesus in His words.

- **Q:** If a Jewish woman was married, in turn, to seven brothers, whose wife would she be in heaven? **A:** "Your problem is, you don't know the Scriptures."

- **Q:** Who gave you authority to do these things? **A:** "Who gave you authority to question me?"

- **Q:** Should we pay the Roman tax to Caesar or not? **A:** "Give to Caesar what is his, and to God what is His."

- **Q:** What is the greatest commandment? **A:** "Love God with everything you've got."

- And Jesus turned the tables on them by stumping them with His Q & A: over and over.

- **THE LESSON:** *You'd better know your stuff if you plan to question the King of kings and Lord of lords.*

in on the "So what?" aspect of preaching. Without application, listeners are left wondering how it actually makes a difference in their daily lives outside the church walls.

How important is application? **"Application is more than just taking the sermon truth and attacking the congregation with it.** Application presents the implications of biblical truth for the contemporary audience. It's a call for action, for putting the principles of Scripture to work in our lives."[31]

A survey of reasons why churchgoers don't like preaching revealed that when knowledge is imparted, but no life application is attached, the preaching is powerless. Jesus knew that and added, in simple words, what the questioner was lacking: *action*.

After using the Navigators 2:7 discipleship series in my ministry, I began to incorporate the regular use of "Life Application" at the end of my messages. Several years later, a visitor to our church asked me, after a sermon, if I had ever used the Navigators' material because she recognized the attention given to applying what we had just heard. Jesus knew that application matters, even before the Navigators incorporated it into their excellent materials.

**The lawyer wanted to "justify" himself.** He asked Jesus, "So, who is my neighbor?" That's actually a very good question, one that Jesus was prepared to answer. In fact this may have been the point Jesus was driving at. As He often did, He told a story (Luke 10:30–35). "And the moral of the story is…"

## SECOND-CLASS CITIZEN OFFERED FIRST-CLASS AID

**Who were the crime-scene avoiders?** To make a long story shorter, we can lump the priest and the Levite together in Jesus's parable. They were bound by similar rules and served the religious community in related

---
[31] www.preaching.com/application

ways. On their way down the road to Jericho they both saw the victim of a mugging and crossed to the other side of the road.

The Law of Moses forbade touching a dead person other than your close kin. In this case, who knew if the victim was even alive? Besides, they may have rationalized, we're busy and important people. Who has time for this inconvenience? And we're not medics. Let the experts take care of him.

For the religious establishment, helping the victim was a lose–lose situation. There was no advantage to be gained by getting involved. Their honor, reputation and pride were more important than the needs of common people. Their choice to move across the road to avoid the problem was symbolically important. "Don't bother us. We have better things to do!"

**What's with these Samaritans?** Samaria was a ghetto between Jerusalem and Galilee. It had been the capital of the ungodly ten tribes of Israel after King Solomon died. For two centuries they struggled in the shadow of Judah, and never once had a godly king. They worshiped Baal and a host of other detestable idols. They sometimes actually burned their children as offerings to Molech and other gods.

Finally, God had enough and sent the bloodthirsty Assyrians to cart away the Israelites. As was their common practice, they also imported people from other nations to Samaria to fill it and make it productive. The Samaritans were the resulting generations of mixed–breed people. Hated by Jews and shunned for their corrupted religion, Samaritans were *persona non grata* to all self–respecting Jews. When the religious leaders were looking for words that would most shame and humiliate Jesus, they called Him "a Samaritan and demon possessed" (John 8:48). Those were the two insults most likely, in their opinions, to paint Jesus as worthless and despicable and worthy of death.

**Why was the Good Samaritan's help so remarkable?** Because he did a godly thing in the face of raw, hateful racism. He stopped to help a Jewish victim of violence. Ironically, the Jewish victim might have rejected the Good Samaritan had he been conscious and able to do so!

> "Go M.A.D.—Make A Difference."
> – Ron Hutchcraft
> https://hutchcraft.com

The good man from the slums showed courage. The robbers could show up again. They were ruthless, and would probably believe they were doing God a favor to attack a hated Samaritan. If they had killed him, no court in Israel would convict them of murder.

Yet, he looked at the half-dead Jew and felt compassion. He went out of his way on this journey through no-man's land to serve the desperately injured victim. The Good Samaritan accepted the cost. He was willing to pay more if the tab went higher.

## WALK A MILE IN OTHER PEOPLE'S SHOES

**Answer your own arrogant question.** After telling His story, Jesus turned to the lawyer and asked him the same question he had arrogantly asked Jesus—He turned the tables again. "Which of these three men was a true neighbor to the victim?" Answer your own question. You know the truth if you're willing to admit it. The despised Samaritan was a better neighbor than the clergymen.

Even after the humiliating turn of events, the lawyer could not bring himself to acknowledge the Samaritan as the hero of the story. When Jesus asked which of the three was the better neighbor, his exact words were, "The one who had mercy on him." Not "the good man from Samaria." Not "The kind Samaritan gentleman who risked it all to help a Jewish victim." No, the true neighbor was, according to the lawyer, the nameless one "who showed mercy."

**Now you know. Go and do the same.** I believe Jesus noticed this racist slight. I believe He was saddened by the stubborn refusal even to identify him as a Samaritan. But He was not quite finished. Always looking to bestow redemption, that was Jesus. Always willing to forgive, to lift up the people around Him, to heal and encourage and rescue.

"Now that you know who your neighbor is, show the same godly character that the Samaritan did. Go and care for those in need. Look for someone you can bless, no matter who they are. Improve the lives of those around you. Make this selfless service a guiding principle in your life. Acknowledge and pursue the betterment of people with your thoughts, words and actions. Keep it "People before pride, possessions, programs or property."

Go M.A.D.—**Make A Difference**.

*No man is an island, entire of itself.*
*Each is a piece of the continent, A part of the main...*
*Each man's death diminishes me, For I am involved in mankind.*
*Therefore, send not to know For whom the bell tolls,*
*IT TOLLS FOR THEE.*
Rev'd John Donne, *FOR WHOM THE BELL TOLLS*

---

### MOMENT OF TRUTH

Set out on a journey to meet the needs of others. Serving unselfishly fulfills the words of Christ, satisfies the soul and makes a difference in a needy, suffering world.

---

**MY PERSONAL JOURNEY:** Jesus, please help me do this to be more aware of the needs around me and to know how to meet them:

_____
_____
_____
_____
_____

- I would describe my past awareness of people around me in need in this way:
  _____
  _____
  _____
  _____

- I've been the recipient of help from an unexpected source, which motivates me to help meet others' needs. ❏ Yes ❏ No

- Here's how I want to go M.A.D., make a difference in someone else's life:
  _____
  _____
  _____
  _____

# 11

# A BOWL OF ROCKY ROAD

### JOURNEY TO OVERCOME OPPOSITION
— Nehemiah —
(Nehemiah 1–6)

## THANKS FOR YOUR HELP, BOLL WEEVIL!

In Enterprise, Alabama, stands one of the most unusual monuments ever built. It honors a little insect that nearly destroyed the livelihoods and cotton economy of the South.

The boll weevil is a beetle that feeds on cotton buds and flowers. Native to Central Mexico, it migrated to the United States in the late 1800s and infested all U.S. cotton–growing areas by the 1920s. Why a monument to so destructive an insect? Because before the boll weevil attacked, every family depended on cotton for their livelihood. When the boll weevil struck, farmers were forced to diversify and began to plant peanuts, among other things. It saved southern agriculture.

The inscription on the monument reads, "In profound appreciation of the Boll Weevil and of what it has done as the Herald of Prosperity, this monument was erected by the Citizens of Enterprise, Coffee County, Alabama." James H. Aughey said, **"God brings men into deep waters not to drown them, but to cleanse them."**

Hardships, challenges and problems often influence what we become. These struggles invade the Kingdom of God, too. But they need not control us. They may change our lives. They may force us to look at life differently. They may propel us on a journey to overcome opposition. They may even turn our world upside down. But by the challenges we face, by our struggle against adversity and problems, God's rich blessings become available to many.

Nehemiah found this to be true, as he made a long trek from Persia to Jerusalem. Thank God for people like Nehemiah. They trust God even as the battle rages around them and life is turned topsy-turvy. What can we learn from this extraordinary leader and his simple faith in God?

## NEHEMIAH'S JOURNEY TO RENEWAL

**Nehemiah had a problem.** Some scholars believe that Nehemiah had never been to Jerusalem; he was born in captivity in Persia. He was a trusted servant of King Artaxerxes I. He tasted the King's wine, itself a dangerous occupation. To get a fix on the date, "the twentieth year of King Artaxerxes" (Nehemiah 2:1) was 455 BC.

Persia had ransacked Jerusalem forty years before. Residents came from Jerusalem to Persia and told Nehemiah about the condition of Jerusalem and the pitiful destitution of the Jewish people. This caused Nehemiah to weep and mourn for his homeland and his fellow-Jews. His grief led him to fast and pray.

**Nehemiah prayed.** In the New International Version, the prayer is 218 words long, only about half used for requests. Besides seeking God's help, Nehemiah repented of his people's sins and his own. He admitted that the Jews' troubles arose because they disobeyed God for centuries.

He had already begun to formulate a strategy. His prayer ended with this simple request: "Hear the prayer of all who delight in You, God, and give me success as I go before the king."

**These are the logistics of the problem.** As the cupbearer, Nehemiah's job was to make sure the food and drink were not poisoned and to serve the king at all times. Sometimes he was there when business was being conducted. So, you can see how important it was for the king to trust his cupbearer.

On this day, the king sensed something was amiss with his valued, trusted servant. Artaxerxes asked what was wrong. It was just the opening Nehemiah had prayed for. Soon, the desperate problem of the Jews' plight was out in the open. The king offered his help, and Nehemiah was off on the journey to renew Jerusalem and lift the people out of their poverty and shame.

The logistics were all arranged by God's mighty hand. Nehemiah received permission to rebuild the walls. He was given an armed escort from the Persian army for the long desert journey. He received written orders from the king to obtain the supplies needed for the project. God gave not only the desire and opportunity to do the work, He also supplied the resources.

**Nehemiah prioritized people ahead of projects, processes, property or programs.** Examine the underlying purpose of this project. Nehemiah's concern was not for the stones and timbers that were burned and broken down. It was not anxiety about the physical condition of the city. He did not care that the scenery of his capital was unappealing. Nehemiah's greatest concern was for the people of Israel.

Note the actual wording. "I questioned [the men who came from Israel] about the Jewish remnant that had survived the exile, and also about Jerusalem. They said to me, 'Those who survived the exile and are back in the province are in great trouble and disgrace. The wall of Jerusalem is broken down...'" (Nehemiah 1:2–3).

Nehemiah's prayer confirmed that he saw through the rubble and grasped the real issue. The people of Israel needed revival and renewal. Rebuilding the wall and erecting new gates was important for safety and "civic pride," but only because it would improve the conditions and lives of the people. He prioritized people ahead of everything else. That's what God does. It raises a penetrating question: **Do you love things and use people? Or, like Nehemiah, do you use things and love people?**

Nehemiah's example is obvious: all the building projects, all the programs, all the work and money we spend on property—it all must be because we love people the way God does!

Nehemiah had what he needed, and he made the journey from Persia to Jerusalem, nearly a thousand miles over burning sands and empty desert. What did he find when he arrived?

## LIVING AT GROUND ZERO

**Nehemiah made an assessment.** He went out into the devastated city secretly, during the night, and found broken down walls, burned gates, debris everywhere, passageways blocked. This was his undercover scouting trip with a local guide to see the problem for himself. What he found was not encouraging. Jerusalem was a wasteland of destroyed walls, falling-down houses and debris everywhere. It must've been like many European cities at the end of World War-II.

Three months after the Nazi surrender, American President Harry S. Truman was headed to Potsdam, a suburb of Berlin, for a conference with Allied leaders. On the way, he took a tour of Berlin in an Army Jeep to see the devastation from the Allied bombing. There was little left standing.

Germany's capital city had been bombed twenty-four times in the five months between November 1943 and March 1944. The bombing continued until Berlin was captured by the Russian army, thirteen months later. By then, the city was reduced to 98 million cubic yards of debris. Each attack involved over a thousand planes and up to four million pounds of bombs.

Half the bridges were destroyed and the underground railway tunnels were flooded. Gas, electricity and water were nonexistent in the central city. Out of 245,000 buildings in Berlin, 50,000 had been destroyed. Half the buildings left were damaged. Eighty thousand city residents had died in the carnage.[32]

Jerusalem's carnage was not on that scale, of course. It happened in 587 BC, without radar, flying bombers and high explosives. But the effect was much the same. Jerusalem was a city in shambles, with devastation everywhere and a decimated population. That's what Nehemiah found when he rode through ground zero in the dark.

**The challenge was immense.** Nehemiah called together the elders of the city. "You see the trouble we have on our hands. Jerusalem lies in ruins; the walls are shattered and the gates are burned. Let's rebuild the walls of Jerusalem so that we will no longer be in disgrace." He also told them about the gracious hand of God upon his endeavor and what the King of Persia had done

---

[32] cf. Photographs of Berlin at the end of the World War II, 1945 - Rare Historical Photos • https://rarehistoricalphotos.com/berlin-end-war 1945

> **BTW**
> - **Return From Exile.** After hundreds of years of warnings from God, the rebellious Jews were sent off to foreign lands as punishment; the Kingdom of Israel in 722 BC; the Kingdom of Judah beginning in 606 BC.
> - God's prophets had predicted the exile of Judah and said it would last seventy years.
> - In 538 BC Cyrus, King of Persia, decreed that the temple in Jerusalem was to be rebuilt. He named Zerubbabel Governor in Israel and over 42,000 people returned from exile.
> - In 458 BC Ezra reinstituted temple worship of God.
> - In 445 BC Nehemiah gained permission from King Artaxerxes to rebuild Jerusalem's walls and make the city safe again. (Dates may differ.)
> - While thousands of Jews returned in the centuries before Christ, many others (perhaps millions) never went back. These were the forefathers of the Jews in almost every country of the world. Finally the nation of Israel was reconstituted in May of 1948.

to help them. Nehemiah called his fellow-Jews to step up to the plate. He implored them to throw their weight behind a renewal effort. This project would remove their disgrace and show once again that they were God's chosen people.

**They forged an agreement.** Immediately, they responded, "Let us start rebuilding." So, they began this good work. You get the sense that there was little persuading needed. The people responded with eagerness and a heart of obedience to God. He left His fingerprints on the whole project as great enthusiasm moved the people forward.

Nehemiah chapter 3 lists those who rebuilt sections of the city wall and the gates. Picture the walls rising, day by day, as they faithfully worked to rebuild. But it was not easy; **many obstacles barred their way.** Success was by no means assured. They soon discovered that technical issues were not their only problems.

## REALITY BITES

**They were working against mockery.** Very soon, reality set in for Nehemiah and his comrades. It was not a pretty sight. The general attitude of God's enemies was succinctly reflected in the defiance of two avowed foes of Israel. When they heard about the progress, "they were very much disturbed that someone had come to promote the welfare of the Israelites."

> **Stumbling blocks can also be stepping stones. Follow God and press on regardless.**

What a revealing statement. The enemy was disturbed because someone cared about the people. Someone had come to help the Jews. First, they mocked Nehemiah and the workers. They ridiculed the effort. "What is this you are doing?" they asked. "Are you rebelling against the king?" Time after time, the enemy sent scornful messages, laughing and mocking the people of Jerusalem. "If even a fox climbed up on what they are building, he would break down their flimsy wall!"

**They were working against intimidation.** When the enemies all around heard that the repairs to Jerusalem's walls had gone ahead and that the gaps were being closed, they were furious. They threatened to come and fight against Jerusalem and stir up trouble within. They planted stories of how they were planning sneak attacks. They intimidated. They bullied. They hoped the threats would discourage the workers. Nothing stopped the workers, however, because, as Nehemiah reported, "We prayed to our God and posted a guard day and night to meet this threat."

The opponents even used trickery to halt the building. Their foes called for a conference, a powwow at a place called—I am not making this up—Ono! They intended to ambush Nehemiah, but he responded, "Oh no, I'm not going." This particular trick was tried four times.

"They were trying to frighten us," Nehemiah observed, "thinking, 'Their hands will get too weak for the work, and it will not be completed.' But I prayed to God, 'Now strengthen my hands.'" Then there was an internal kind of problem.

**They were working with inferior materials:** King Artaxerxes gave timber to Nehemiah for rebuilding the gates and some structures. Mostly what they used, however, was damaged goods left from the formerly great city. Not a good situation.

Imagine using the rubble from the World Trade Center in a rebuilding project. It would cause many construction problems. Inferior materials spell trouble on any building project. That's pretty much what Nehemiah and his people faced. How could they do the job right when good stone for the walls was simply not available? Their nemesis, Sanballat, scoffed, "Can they bring the stones back to life from those heaps of rubble—burned as they are?" No, they could not. But God could. And did.

Besides all this, the strength of the people waned; their determination wavered. When you do God's work, this is a danger you may face.

Strength seems to fade, and there is so much to do that you feel overwhelmed. A builder no less capable than King Solomon observed, "Unless the Lord builds the house, its builders labor in vain. Unless the Lord watches over the city, the watchmen stand guard in vain" (Psalm 127:1).

Nehemiah knew this truth. He trusted God to accomplish what the people could not, in their own strength. And, of course, God didn't let them down. They were building with God's strength and wisdom. They finished in just fifty-two days—it was a miracle. Nehemiah triumphantly announced, "When all our enemies heard about this, the surrounding nations were afraid and lost their self-confidence. They could see that this work had been done with the help of our God" (Nehemiah 6:16).

## GOD BLESS THIS JOURNEY

**Remember your purpose.** I don't know your specific project or plan or your exact problem. Nor do I know the challenges that complicate your life. But I do know that God is strong enough to carry you through. Remember your real purpose; not just the project or plan, but the people it can touch and the lives it can change.

**Stay focused on what really counts—people.** God will help us surmount our obstacles if we focus on His people. Our primary goal isn't the plans, projects or properties. It's not nicer facilities, more profit, or a smoother operation. The ultimate goal of God's Kingdom is for people to come to faith in Jesus Christ and then grow into healthy, mature disciples. God will always bless this journey of renewal because it's what He cares about most.

**Recognize the enemy.** Famous Dutch Christian Corrie ten Boom once said, "The first step on the way to victory is to recognize the enemy."

After the Battle of Lake Erie in 1813, Commodore Oliver Perry sent this dispatch, "We have met the enemy and he is ours." Generations later, American satire writer Walter Kelly amended it to read, "We have met the enemy and he is us." To you I say, "We have met the enemy, and he is among us." But defeat is not a foregone conclusion. Like Nehemiah, we can **pray and prepare and step out in vigorous faith.** If we trust God and hold true to our purpose of blessing others for Christ, we may lose a battle here and there, but we cannot lose the war of the ages.

---

### MOMENT OF TRUTH

God can turn your struggles and obstacles into ladders, lifting you to success. Trust Him and keep on climbing.

---

**MY PERSONAL JOURNEY:** A plan, project or process I'm struggling with is:

_____
_____
_____
_____
_____

- This plan, project or process is: ❑ people–focused ❑ self–focused

- The obstacle holding me back is

_____
_____
_____
_____
_____

- I'm seeking God to help overcome the obstacle in this way:

_____
_____
_____

## Nehemiah's Top–20 Leadership Principles

Nehemiah . . .

1. Established reasonable, attainable goals.
2. Had a sense of God-given mission.
3. Was willing to get involved, even in hardships.
4. Arranged priorities to accomplish goals (people first).
5. Waited patiently for God's timing.
6. Respected his superiors.
7. Prayed at crucial times.
8. Made his requests with tact and grace.
9. Was well-prepared and thought of needs in advance.
10. Went through proper channels.
11. Took time to rest, pray and plan.
12. Investigated the situation firsthand.
13. Informed others only after identifying the problem.
14. Identified himself as one of the people.
15. Established reasonable goals for the workers.
16. Assured the people that God was in the project.
17. Displayed God's confidence in facing obstacles.
18. Established self-confidence in facing obstacles.
19. Did not argue with opponents.
20. Was not discouraged by opponents.

# 12

# A TALE OF TWO FRIENDSHIPS

**JOURNEY TO MUTUAL RELATIONSHIPS**
— The Shunammite Woman —
(2 Kings 4:8–36)

In his novel, *A Tale of Two Cities,* set in late eighteenth–century London and Paris, Charles Dickens tells a story of unexpected friendship. Exiled French Marquis Charles Darnay has fallen in love with Lucie Manette. Immoral and self–indulgent British lawyer Sydney Carton is also attracted to the Doctor's lovely daughter.

Carton has seen his once–promising life atrophy through selfishness, dissipation, alcohol and other evils. Seeing the two men together, someone observes that Carton and Darnay look like identical twins. At first, the two men are suspicious of each other—and hostile. They're jealous for the affections of Lucie. Eventually, Darnay gains the advantage and wins her affections. They are married and begin a family. As time passes, Carton begins to display a nascent moral and ethical compass. He vows to make any sacrifice necessary to benefit Lucie and those she loves, including his one–time rival, her husband Darnay.

The French Revolution is raging. No one is immune to the guillotine. The mere suggestion of treason against the rebellion could chop your head off into a bloody basket. Making a secret journey to Paris to help a family friend detained in the Bastille, Darnay is himself arrested. Eventually, he is convicted of treason and condemned to die.

The night before the grisly public execution, Carton slips into the prison and trades places with Darnay, his double. The grateful Marquis escapes to freedom. Carton feels his life has been worthless and wasted. By taking Darnay's punishment he believes he can make amends for his corrupt life. He sacrifices himself to the guillotine because he knows the survival of Lucie's beloved will bring her great joy. Hence, Carton's famous declaration, "It is a far, far better thing that I do, than I have ever done; it is a far, far better rest that I go to than I have ever known."

Carton's chivalry is not exactly the expected response to the rivalry between two competitors for a beautiful woman. But friendships spring up in surprising places and in some of the most unforeseen circumstances. As Ralph Waldo Emerson observed, "God evidently does not intend us all to

---

**BTW**

- **Agribusiness** was the main source of wealth in Elisha's day.
- Socio–economic ranking was done by tallying the land, livestock, stored agricultural produce and number of servants a landowner employed.
- This couple was well off, judging by the busy farming life, the hospitality they offered Elisha and by the costly building of the "prophet's room" where Elisha often spent a night in their care.
- Culturally, the offer of hospitality and protection to a guest was a sacred responsibility. If someone was sheltered under your roof, you were expected to provide for them even at great cost or risk to you.
- Read Genesis 19 to see the extremes of this obligation in Lot's home in Sodom.
- **THE LESSON:** *The spiritual gift of hospitality figures prominently in the New Testament church. In fact, the writer of Hebrews claims that some have shared this gift with angels (Hebrews 13:2).*

be rich, or powerful, or great, but he does intend us all to be friends."[33]

An unusual friendship from the Bible shows us how God often uses relationships, even unpredictable ones, to bring healing and wholeness. It will teach us to build and nourish friendships for their reciprocal value, for mutual benefit and for the blessings one friendship can bring to both sides.

In this biblical account, a friendship grows between a prophet of God and a childless couple who has befriended him. Nowhere are the names revealed. The woman is simply called the Shunammite.

## A FRIENDSHIP ESTABLISHED

**It was an act of kindness.** As Elisha, God's prophet, passed through the village of Shunem, a prosperous woman offered him a meal. And she suggested to her husband that they make a small apartment where Elisha could stay when he was in town. As Motel-6® used to say, "The light is always on." Thus, a relationship emerged.

The practice of building friendships over a plate of food didn't begin in the country churches of the American South. It predates the potluck dinner by millennia. The act of kindness was done, and Elisha was blessed by their growing friendship. It increased because of the hospitality of this kindly couple. Over time, the prophet and the couple became close friends.

Emerson called friendship "a sheltering tree." So it was for the faithful man of God, Elisha. Friendship became a tree whose shade was cast by the thoughtfulness of this agrarian couple. They didn't do these things simply to get something they wanted. They were being genuinely friendly. Apparently, there was no selfishness, no ulterior motive involved.

## A FRIENDSHIP MUTUALLY BENEFICIAL

**Genuine friendship is always reciprocal.** As the friendship blossomed,

---
[33] www.idlehearts.com/2085180/god-evidently-does-not

Elisha felt the desire to reciprocate. He said, "You've gone to all this trouble for me. What can I do for you?" Kindness breeds kindness, and he wanted to bless the couple as they had blessed him. The Shunammite responded, "I have everything I need." But that didn't satisfy Elisha's desire to express his gratitude. He pressed the point.

His servant, Gehazi, observed that the couple had no children, a tragic situation in that culture. With God's permission, we can assume, Elisha promised her a son. Her response was sadly predictable, "Please don't get my hopes up after all these years of trying!" But God was faithful and kept His promise. In due time, a treasured son was born to the grateful couple.

**Every coin has two sides.** This story beautifully depicts the principle of relational mutuality: "Friendship goes two ways." If it doesn't, it won't last. If it's not mutual, is it even friendship? A one-way journey of friendship cannot reach the destination of mutual benefit. You can't get there from here!

Aristotle once said, "A friend is a single soul dwelling in two bodies!" Emerson (again) opined that friendship is like a bank account. You cannot continue to draw on it without making deposits.

The compassion of the Shunammite couple (building a cozy room for Elisha's comfort) resulted in mutual kindness (God's promise of a son is fulfilled). But almost every life has its crises.

## FRIENDSHIP IN TIME OF CRISIS

No calamity galvanizes parents like their children in danger. The Shunammite couple was no different. The boy apparently got sunstroke in the field with his father. Later, the lad of God's promise died in his mother's arms. She knew that her friendship with Elisha might make a difference, so she seized on that in her distress. Their mutual friendship permitted the mother to ask for and receive assistance.

She made a mad dash to the prophet. Her journey was an ambulance chase at high speed, with siren shrieking. She was single-minded in her purpose. The journey was a desperate one, and she hit the road at a dead-run.

As the Bible reveals, her dependence on a trusted friend resulted in perhaps an even bigger blessing than overcoming barrenness. Her son was soon restored to life.

**Friends often have needed resources.** Elisha had a source of help the mother didn't have. He had a prophetic connection with the God of Israel, Who could do anything. She wasn't hesitant to draw on that reserve in her time of great need. Hers was a journey of hope, based on her confidence in a special friendship. When an alliance is structured around mutual faith in God, it becomes an unstoppable force, an immovable object.

## FRIENDSHIP LESSONS FROM ELISHA

**Nurture mutual friendships.** There are always two elements in friendship. For one thing, how do I benefit? Equally important, how can I bless my friend? Ask yourself, "How can I strengthen this friendship? What can I do to bless my friend?" Inquire of God, "Why have You brought us together as friends? What can we do for each other?"

**Find resources you don't have from the friends in your life.** No one is self-contained, needing nothing or no one. Peter Marshall wrote, "Small deeds done are better than great deeds planned." *Duck Dynasty's* Willie Robertson makes the point, "God created us to thrive on encouragement from others."[34]

> Relationships that go the distance take every aspect of human life into consideration, mental-emotional, physical, spiritual and social.

You have needs you cannot meet by yourself, as the Shunammite woman did. Matching needs with resources is a gift God gives some

---
[34] www.pinterest.com/pin/364087951099801144

people. If you're one of those people, look for ways to cultivate your ability. God is eager to employ those who put resources and needs together.

Look for ways to meet others' needs. Keep the principle of *mutual relationships* in mind as you practice friendship. Be a "need–meeter" who thinks about how to bless and benefit your friends. Be intentional; be reciprocal. Don't allow a friendship to become lopsided. Ideally, the journey to friendship culminates in mutual blessings to both sides.

Close friendships can strengthen, encourage and guide people in times of great need. Build quality mutual relationships that will bless both ways in times of need.

Jay Kesler, former President of Youth for Christ, writes, "One of my goals in life is to wind up with eight men who are willing to carry one of my handles."[35] It is his quaint way of saying he wants to make many friendships.

It goes beyond cultivating pallbearers. We can move to a more profound level of friendship. It's a plane where a few people care enough about you, and you about them, to show two–way friendship while you're all still alive. Be determined to bless each other through the journeys of life, in times of pain and seasons of pleasure.

---

**MOMENT OF TRUTH**

Relationship building is vital if friendships are to be two–way streets of mutual benefit. Build solid relationships that can meet mental–emotional, physical, spiritual and social needs for everyone.

---

MY PERSONAL JOURNEY: One time when God blessed me through a reciprocal friendship was:

_____

---

[35] Jay Kesler, *Being Holy Being Human: Dealing With the Incredible Expectations and Pressures of Ministry*. Minneapolis: Bethany House Publishers, 1994

# A TALE OF TWO FRIENDSHIPS

_____
_____
_____
_____

- The average level of my friendships is:

  | 0 | 1 | 2 | 3 | 4 | 5 | 6 | 7 | 8 | 9 | 10 |
  |---|---|---|---|---|---|---|---|---|---|----|
  | Rock–bottom | | | | | About average | | | | | Sky high |

- I practice the principle of mutual relationship with at least ___ others.

- Here's how a mutual friendship has blessed my life:
_____
_____
_____
_____
_____

- Here is a one–sided friendship that brought trouble to my life:
_____
_____
_____
_____

- I have seen friendships that became lopsided. I will do this if it happens to me:
_____
_____

_____

_____

_____

- I am going on record that I want to develop mutual friendships that bless both sides. ❐ Yes ❐ No

# 13

# HOME WHERE YOU BELONG

---

**JOURNEY TO RECONCILIATION**
— The Prodigal Father —
(Luke 15:11–24)

Many families have confrontations, disagreements, harsh words and conflict. Something has divided family members. Usually, the trigger is not huge, just the "last straw" after other unpleasant things have occurred.

For whatever reason, feelings are hurt, people get defensive, things are said, and before you know it, one person refuses to speak to another. Or they harbor the hurt deep inside, where it metastasizes into a seeping wound that can poison a life.

The result is kids who won't talk to their parents, brothers and sisters at odds, families fractured and divided and alienated from each other. It may have been so long ago that the details are lost in the fog.

I remember being faintly angry at my mother–in–law, a godly woman with strong opinions. My wife sometimes had issues with her, and I could get caught up in them, if only on the fringe. Kathy and her mom remained connected, never really alienated. But they had baggage, like many mother–daughter relationships. And I wasn't always savvy enough to keep my trap shut.

As we were leaving on a date once, her mom said to her, "Have a good time!" to which Kathy replied, "Don't tell me what to do!"

The Bible has stories like that too. In Genesis, Abraham and his nephew Lot had trouble sharing space. There wasn't enough for both growing families and mushrooming businesses. So, they divided and went their separate ways. It probably saved their long-term friendship. You can read in 2 Samuel about the terrible tragedies in David's family: rape, murder, rebellion. And that was one of the better families, in some respects.

Jesus told a story about a man and his son who had a major split. This might be the most popular parable in Scripture since so many of us can relate to it. It's called The Prodigal Son. In this chapter, I call it "The Prodigal Father." Not because the Old Man was in the wrong, but because we all can learn such an important lesson about being parents, or being sons or daughters, from this father's journey.

The son took two long journeys, one to run away from home, the other to come crawling back. But the most important journey in this parable is a short one that The Prodigal Father made when he saw his wayward son coming home. In every life...

## SHIFT HAPPENS

**Father and son had a falling out.** Inheritances can produce raised temperatures. We don't know the underlying cause of their problem. Apparently, there was strife between father and son. The falling out came to a head when the young man demanded his inheritance while his father was still alive. This was like saying, "Old Man, I wish you were already dead, so I could start spending your money!" Jesus's listeners understood this point.

Would you feel hurt if one of your children said that? Of course you would, and rightly so. But the father in Jesus's parable kept his cool and agreed to the selfish, mean-spirited scheme. He was thinking long-term, not simply the immediate present.

The son ran off and quickly blew through his inheritance. He wasted his father's hard-earned money on wild living. Then, he hit bottom. The money was gone. The friends disappeared. The party was over. Famine encroached. Hunger gnawed at him like a starving rat. The boy, who had been a rich man's son all his life, was suddenly desperate. Now and then, life throws us a huge shift.

**Circumstances change.** When parents and children become alienated, sooner or later, the circumstances change in some way—sometimes in big ways. In this parable, the young man soon found himself destitute. He was unprepared for that unfamiliar condition.

The Jewish boy was so hungry that he took a job feeding pigs. He even ate their food! When his growling stomach drowned out the sounds of the despised porkers eating around him, he knew something had to change.

## BTW

- **DYSFUNCTIONAL FAMILIES.** The Bible tells it like it is, even when it ain't pretty.

- The very first dysphoric family was probably Adam's and Eve's, where rebellion cast the human race into chaos, and where the first son murdered his younger brother.

- Isaac loved his firstborn Esau, while Rebekah favored Jacob. It led to tension you could cut with a dull butter knife.

- Then there was Jacob's family, with two wives, two concubines and twelve sons, of whom Joseph was the clear favorite. Jealousy swamped the entire family and led to mayhem.

- Even Bible hero David had lots of turmoil. Not only did he sleep with the woman next door, his son Absalom tried to kill him and take over the kingdom.

- **THE LESSON:** *Even in families that bless the world, problems seem to multiply like mold. Only the intervention of God can calm the waters and keep us sane.*

- "Lord, give me wisdom to guide my loved ones to lives of faith and effectiveness. Amen!"

He swallowed his pride and came skulking home. Some of life's journeys are hard enough. But when you find yourself crawling, it can be intolerable.

"Father," he explained, "I have sinned against heaven and against you. I am no longer worthy to be called your son" (Luke 15:21). Right you are. He didn't deserve to be an heir. He probably gritted his teeth and prepared himself for a tongue–lashing—or worse.

**Dad's response was a surprise.** The best part of the whole story has less to do with the Prodigal Son and everything to do with the Prodigal Father. He was waiting on the front porch, as he often did. His love and sadness compelled him to watch and long for his wayward boy. Even his previous humiliation at his hands did not stymie the yearning. He saw the young man while he was still a long way off. And love overpowered his pride and hurt.

> **Family love over-shadows many a slight, insult or offense. The journey to relational healing requires an unselfish decision to extend grace.**

He hiked up his long robe, and with proper Jewish dignity cast to the wind, he dashed to the wastrel child he loved. This was his short but life–changing journey of reconciliation.

Standing there in the middle of the dusty road, the prodigal father threw his arms around the young man, who then started his rehearsed speech. "Father, I do not deserve to be called your son. Make me your servant instead…"

Many rejections could have come to the father's lips. What might he have said to his son? Put yourself in his sandals.

"Get off my land; you're dead to me!"

"I told you this would turn out badly, you miserable failure!"

"So–o–o, how do you like feeding pigs?"

"Sure, you can be a hired man. Go clean my toilet!"

"Pay back all my money before you even think of being my son again!"

"Where are all your floozy friends now? Let *them* feed you!"

He might have taken a different approach and tried to make the whole sorry mess disappear. Just sweep it under the rug.

"Forget about it, son. Act like it never happened!"

"Oh, that's okay. Don't worry about it!"

"It was all my fault, boy. I take the blame."

The beauty of this story, however, is the Old Man's actual handling of the scandal. Ignoring the son's self-condemnation, he ordered his servants, "Quick! Bring the best clothes for him. Put a ring with the family crest on his finger and good shoes on his feet. Bring a plump calf and fix it for dinner. Let's have a feast and celebrate. For this son of mine was dead but is alive again. He was lost but now he is found. Let the party begin" (Luke 15:22–24).

He didn't excuse the bad behavior. Neither did he berate, reject, or humiliate him. He believed the relationship was more important than money, decorum or pride. He was simply overcome by a father's love. It trumped payback, rejection, anger and pride. Having him back exceeded any thought of revenge he may have entertained.

**Don't get historical.** A wife complained to her friend that whenever she argued with her husband he got all *historical* on her. Her friend said, 'You mean *hysterical*.' She said, 'No, *historical*. He dredges up the past and reminds me of every time I ever failed him.'"

Sometimes people do that with their children too. The kids do something wrong; they let their parents down, embarrass them, or fail in some way. So the parents push them away and remind them how often they've been disappointed in them. We can only hope this father and son didn't perpetuate that vicious cycle.

"***Justice*** is getting what you deserve. ***Mercy*** is not getting what you deserve. **Grace** is getting what you absolutely do not deserve."[36] All three qualities impact relationships beyond words.

The Prodigal Son deserved justice but received mercy from his father. You and I have received mercy from God too. We have many reasons to dispense it to others.

## WHAT HAPPENS TO STUFF THAT HAPPENED?

What should you do with whatever has happened between you and your loved ones? What happened is past; you cannot deny it, undo it, or change it. But how you respond to it is critically important. Don't say, "I can't help it." or "I can't do anything about it!" The power to do the right thing is within you, as God gives wisdom and strength. Love compels us to forgive. But it doesn't require that we make a practice of being trampled. Pray, show mercy, and be realistic.

**Our decisions have long-term consequences, too.** The long-term always matters more than the short-term. Life is a marathon, not a sprint. Do whatever it takes to keep rifts from becoming continental, generational alienation. Sometimes, we have to swallow our pride. Sometimes we have to say...

- the two hardest words: "I'm sorry."
- the three hardest words: "I forgive you." Or, "Please forgive me."
- the four hardest words: "Let's work this out."
- the five hardest words: "You really matter to me."
- the six hardest words: "You were right; I was wrong!" (My least favorite).

Of course, there are the twenty-two hardest words: *"You're more important than any argument, expense, inconvenience, or matter of pride. Our relationship is too important to be alienated by this."*

I've heard, and said, too many hurtful things to be wrong about this. There are long-term consequences to the decisions you make about

---

[36] Cathleen Falsani, *Sin Boldly: A Field Guide for Grace*. Grand Rapids: Zondervan. 2008

the stuff that happens in life. Don't let the short-term devour the long-term. If you don't take good care of your relationships, the fallout can last the rest of your life—or even beyond. You may be eternally sorry for the decision you made about stuff that won't matter in eternity.

**God cares about what happened.** Making good decisions about conflict is important to you, of course. But also important to the other people in your life. Decisions can impact innocent people around you.

Above all, our decisions matter to God. He sent His Son to heal the biggest rift, the worst alienation of them all: the fall of humanity into sin and separation from God.

The story of the Prodigal Father is all about what God does when you and I rebel and walk away. When we come back, God virtually runs to us. He embraces us. He says, "Put on new clothing, wear this ring and eat the best My chef can make. Let's rejoice because you went missing, but now you're found!"

What a great example for everyone, especially parents and their children. Put the other person and reconciliation ahead of your hurts, pride and selfish desires. Do whatever it takes to heal relationships and bless your family. That's the journey to interpersonal healing. It has eternal implications!

---

**MOMENT OF TRUTH**

When love wins over hurt, forgiveness and reconciliation are possible.

---

**MY PERSONAL JOURNEY:** Someone with whom I need to mend fences:

_____

_____

- The problem we need to work through is:

_____

- How can I contribute to harmony with this person?

- "Lord, I know that You're all about reconciliation. Help me accept the ministry of reconciliation (2 Corinthians 5:17–21) in this way":

# 14

# THE GREAT DETOUR

**JOURNEY TO TRANSFORMATION**
— Saul who became Paul —
(Acts 8:1–3; 9:1–31; 22:4–5)

## LIFE'S DRIVING FORCE IN A NUTSHELL

They can now use lasers to etch detailed pictures on tombstones. I've seen leaping fish, bountiful gardens, hunters of big game, and my personal favorite, tables loaded with delicious foods. Tombstones may include brief poems about family ties, religious faith, loyalty to one's country, or a favorite branch of the military. An occasional Bible verse is included.

When they chisel (or laser) your tombstone, will it hint about what powered your life? Is there one overarching principle that shapes everything you do and defines your existence? Some people are born, live and die, and no one (including themselves, perhaps) has a clue to the passion that drove them. Others' motivation is clear at a glance. Of course, some live passionless lives. How sad.

One Bible character had an all-consuming passion for what he did in life. Saul was a Pharisee born in Tarsus, today's southern Turkey. He grew up at the feet of the great Jewish Rabbi, Gamaliel, in Jerusalem.

**Saul was a rabid enemy of Jesus.** The driving force guiding his life was "Destroy the church." He "breathed out murderous threats" against the Lord's disciples and took road trips in his zeal to stamp out "The Way," as the early church was known. He was an existential threat to believers, well-known throughout the church. He was feared by Christians, but revered by Jewish purists.

We find Saul (better known as Paul, cf. Acts 13:9) riding the road to Damascus, the ancient Syrian city. He was surrounded by followers, petty officials and guards from the Jewish priests. He was pursuing Christians, running them to earth and arresting them. Some would lose their lives as a result. He was on a 'holy' mission for the High Priest, a journey to defend Moses's Law from the latest religious cult. And he was passionate about his mission.

## FANGS BECOME FAITH

**Heavenly light illuminated the Savior to the killer.** As Saul neared Damascus on his journey to mayhem, an intense light illuminated the road. It was like staring into the sun. Even in broad daylight it penetrated clenched eyelids and crisped vulnerable retinas. It slammed the caravan to a halt and shattered his vision. He fell to the ground as a voice rocked his world: "Saul, why are you persecuting Me?" The first thing Saul could say was, "Who are you, Lord?" The voice replied, "I am Jesus, Whom you are persecuting."

Saul certainly recognized the name. He had pursued many people who worshiped this blasphemous interloper. This was the enemy!

Jesus continued, "Go into the city and wait to be told what to do." When the voice stopped, Saul opened his eyes to discover he was blinded by the light. They took his hand and led him to his destination. For three days Saul was blind and did not eat or drink anything. Instead, he prayed nonstop. Saul's journey to transformation had begun.

**God used a reluctant deliverer.** Meanwhile, Jesus was not idle while Saul sat in darkness, fearing the future. The Lord spoke to a disciple named Ananias in a vision. "Go to the house of Judas on Straight Street and ask for Saul. He's praying and waiting for you to place your hands on him. Then he will see again."

As you might expect, Ananias had immediate call reluctance. Believers were scrambling to get out of Saul's way. Keeping away from him was a matter of life and death. No doubt his journey to Damascus was well-known. Christians were in all-out fight-or-flight mode—mostly *flight!*

"Lord, we've all heard about this man and the harm he has done to the Jerusalem church. He has come here with similar intentions. I'm terrified of him, yet You want me to go and anoint him for healing? What's wrong with this picture?"

Ananias was clueless about the future God had in mind. There's a stark demarcation between fear and trust in God. Like many of us, Ananias couldn't figure out where God was going with this. But he also believed he could trust the Lord.[37] He was seeking clarification.

"Do as I say," Jesus reassured him. "This man is my chosen instrument for spreading the Gospel, both to Jews and Gentiles. He will suffer terribly for My name."

Many journeys begin with a measure of trepidation. Fear is a powerful emotion. Am I understanding God clearly? What if I have my signals crossed? **Why would God ask me to do this wild and crazy thing?** But wait. Jesus always guides me on His preferred path. He always has my back. He knows what's best. I'm going to trust Him and step out in faith. I will do what I believe He has called me to do. The final result is up to Him.

---

[37] Find YouTube: He's Been Faithful – Brooklyn Tabernacle Choir

## FOLLOW THE DETOUR SIGNS

> Saul's detour took him on a whole new journey to God's preferred future.

The telltale sign of Ananias's faith lurks in the words he speaks to Saul. He calls him "Brother Saul." The Lord Jesus has sent me to you, he explains. He wants to make you see again. And more importantly, *He's going to fill you with the Holy Spirit*.

Annanias laid his hands on Saul's eyes and the scales that were blinding Saul fell away. His vision was restored. He was baptized into faith in Jesus Christ. So proceeded his amazing, life–altering detour.

**Relinquish operational control.** A simple, illiterate Londoner was transformed from alcoholic to believer through the work of the Salvation Army. He went every Sunday to the Salvationists' chapel. One day he came home upset. His wife asked, "What's the matter?"

He said, "I've just noticed that all the Salvation Army people wear red sweaters, and I don't have a red sweater."

She said, "I can fix that." So she knitted him a red sweater, which he wore proudly to chapel the next Sunday. Returning home, he was still unhappy. His wife asked, "What's wrong this time?" He replied, "I just noticed that all their red sweaters have some yellow writing on them, three words long."

She had trouble reading but she said, "Don't worry about it. I'll embroider some words on it for you." She had no idea what the yellow writing on the red sweater of the Salvation Army said. It was actually, "Blood and Fire." That's their motto. Copying a handy sign from a store window across the street, she embroidered three words in yellow thread onto his red sweater.

When he came home next Sunday, she asked, "Did they like your sweater?"

"They loved it," he beamed. "Some of them said they liked my sweater better than their own."

# THE GREAT DETOUR

What this humble yet faithful couple didn't know was that the sign in the store window across the street said, **"Under New Management."** What a great thing for a person to proclaim: "My life is under new management."

**It's the best sort of detour.** We can declare that same message in our own lives! It means giving up the precious control we think we have in life. But do any of us really control very much at all about life? I've found that relinquishing control to a loving and trustworthy God is safer, and for that matter, much more effective than trying to be in control myself.

Under New Management, that's what Saul's sweater could have said! He was being transformed, before their very eyes, by the power of Jesus, Whom he had so hated. The passion that drove his life had turned 180 degrees. BTW, that's the perfect definition of *repentance*.

## A LONG, PRODUCTIVE LIFE OF USEFUL MINISTRY

All that stood between the old Saul "of murderous intent" and the new

> **BTW**
>
> - **Paul** was the world's first missionary. He dedicated his life to founding Christian churches in the Roman Empire and across the known world of that time.
>
> - First missionary journey (Acts 13–14) included the island of Cyprus and Asia Minor (now Turkey). They were heavily persecuted by the local Jews.
>
> - Second missionary journey (Acts 15:36–18:22). Before leaving Syria, Paul and Barnabas argued over taking John Mark with them, and chose different ministry partners. Paul and Silas found Timothy in Lystra, then northwest toward the line where Asia becomes Europe. Arriving in Troas (ancient Troy), a vision steered the missionaries to Thessalonika, Athens, Corinth and Ephesus.
>
> - Third missionary journey (Acts 18:23–21:14). Back to Ephesus, Greece and Turkey, where they revisited established churches and won many productive converts to The Way. Then Paul went to a Roman prison.

Paul of bold service to his Savior, Jesus, seems to have been a quick meal to regain his strength. "*At once* he began to preach that Jesus is the Son of God," says Luke in Acts 9:20. And all who heard him were astonished.

**Is there a wolf among the sheep?** As so often with miraculous conversions, people were skeptical of Saul—and cautious. They knew his backstory. A residue of suspicion stubbornly remained. Some said, in effect, "Hold on a minute. This guy raised havoc with our sisters and brothers in Jerusalem. And he came here to Damascus specifically to arrest believers and drag us back to the Chief Priest. It doesn't seem prudent to trust him."

Yet Luke records that Saul grew ever more powerful in service to Jesus. In fact, he "baffled the Jews living in Damascus." He did that by "proving that Jesus is the Messiah." Think about that for a moment.

**Who is this promised Messiah?** The Messiah for whom the Jews were waiting and watching was expected to be a political, even a military deliverer for the Jews. The hated Romans were the world power of their day. Devout Jews expected their promised Messiah to overthrow every oppressor and restore the theistic rule of God in political matters. And, contrary to the current Palestinian narrative, the Jews had history on their side.

In their distant past, God had delivered them from Pharaoh and birthed a nation guided by Moses's law. Later, the judges and kings of Israel and Judah threw off the yoke of oppression and returned God to the throne—endless overlapping cycles of obey, disobey, suffer, cry out for help, and obey again, followed by a familiar repeat...

After the Dispersion (Israel in exile by the Assyrians, Babylonians and Persians), Ezra rebuilt the temple and Nehemiah rebuilt the wall of Jerusalem. Order, civilization and worship were restored to Zion.

In the two hundred years before Jesus's birth, the Maccabees had started a revolt against the tyrant Antiochus Epiphanes and freed Jerusalem from Greek tyranny. Then slowly, over the next century, the

Roman Empire washed, like a relentless storm surge, over Palestine. By Jesus's day, Rome ruled with their infamous iron fist. Their coming Messiah was supposed to throw off the chains, they believed, and free the Jews for self-rule. He would bring a religious component, sure. But in Jewish minds, his primary purpose was to return political power to Jewish control.

And now this Pharisee–turned–Christian, Saul of Tarsus, was proving the Messiahship of Jesus by using the Scriptures. Oh, wait! The only Bible of that time was the Law and Prophets and books of Poetry comprising the Hebrew Tanakh. So, we have this dedicated scholar of Judaism, proving with the Old Testament, no less, that Jesus Christ, the crucified and resurrected Son of God, is the people's Messiah.

**Grace is Good News.** In his own stellar way, Philip Yancey writes, "When I ask my airplane seatmates, 'What comes to mind when I say the words 'evangelical Christian'? they usually respond in political terms. Yet the gospel of Jesus was not primarily a political platform. In all the talk of voting blocs and culture wars, the message of grace—the main distinctive [that] Christians have to offer—tends to fall aside. It is difficult, if not impossible, to communicate the message of grace from the corridors of power."[38]

The apostle Paul began all his letters with a prayer for God's grace extended to his readers. More than anything else, grace characterized his message to the world. **Grace is all God's blessings we do not deserve and cannot earn.**

Saul was obviously growing more and more powerful as a Christian leader. His preaching roiled the waters and upset the status quo. He used the authority of Scripture to answer questions that had hung in the air for seven hundred years. In a matter of days the Jews' star player became their biggest foe.

---

[38] Philip Yancey, *What's So Amazing About Grace?* Grand Rapids: Zondervan. ePub format. 1997. p. 230

Today, the church seems more politicized than at any time since the Popes ruled Europe. Yet, following Jesus's example and Saul's approach, our message of grace and spiritual transformation is the only hope for the world.

**Saul's sudden U-turn made his former colleagues turn on him.** Before many days passed, Saul learned that the Damascus Jews were hatching a plot to kill him. They were lying in wait, hoping for an opportunity to give him a dose of his own murderous medicine. But with the help of Jesus's disciples, he went over the wall in a basket and escaped. A similar kind of thing happened years later in Jerusalem. It would result in Paul declaring the Gospel before the very ramparts of Rome.

**Saul won friends and influenced people.** Apparently, when he returned to Jerusalem from Damascus, word of his conversion lagged behind. When he tried to join the apostles in Jerusalem, they were fearful, doubting his loyalty to Jesus. Barnabas, who would become Paul's partner in missionary work, spoke up for him. "He told them how Saul on his journey had seen the Lord" and explained that he had "preached fearlessly in the name of Jesus."

Soon, Saul was boldly proclaiming the good news of the Gospel and even debating the Jewish authorities. After another attempt on his life, the believers sent him home to Tarsus, where he was safe. And the church enjoyed a time of peace and growth.

**Saul's journey to transformation is everyone's journey.** A crucial element lacking in many people's Christian experience is the fact that **trusting Jesus as Savior demands real, permanent change.** It presents a detour from selfish living (our default setting) to surrender to Christ's kind of life.

A full range of outcomes after a conversion includes **those who take on the name of Jesus but few or none of His characteristics or attitudes.** Others are like the seed in Jesus's parable in Luke 8:4–15. Some are tested and their faith proves shallow and feeble. Some are genuinely repentant, but then are consumed by the cares, worries and riches of life and fail to mature.

**Only those who believe and are willing to surrender control of their own lives to Christ (in other words, to *change*) will grow into healthy, productive believers** who grow a harvest of godliness. This challenging detour from life as usual will change the entire course of your life and many others you influence.

"If you want people to change, tell them about Jesus!" Saul/Paul is the quintessential example of this principle. This change, this transformation, led him to a lifetime of godly service that has endured and blessed the Body of Christ for two millennia.

"The old has gone, the new has come" is surely the concept distilled from Paul's words in 2 Corinthians 5:17. It was a reality in his life, and it became his passionate motivation for the rest of his days. Sounds intriguing, huh?

---

**MOMENT OF TRUTH**

'Murderous intent' can become lifelong service if you follow the detour signs Jesus puts up on your journey through life.

---

**MY PERSONAL JOURNEY:** My story of transformation at the hands of Jesus is:

_____
_____
_____
_____
_____

- How effectively am I surrendering my control to Jesus?

  | 0 | 1 | 2 | 3 | 4 | 5 | 6 | 7 | 8 | 9 | 10 |
  |---|---|---|---|---|---|---|---|---|---|----|
  | I'm firmly in charge | | | | | Still learning to let go | | | | | God's in charge |

- I still need to follow God's detour in my life in this area:

  _____
  _____
  _____
  _____

- According to Luke 8:4–15, I am this kind of 'seed':

  _____
  _____
  _____
  _____

# 15

# HUMBLE HIGHWAY

**JOURNEY TO HEALING HUMILITY**
— Naaman —
(2 Kings 5:1–19)

Having spent many years ministering in Illinois, I find it interesting that the Indian word "Illini" means "tribe of superior men." I saw a person at Epcot Center wearing a Florida State University T-shirt that read, "We're not arrogant. We really are better than you."

Throughout history, many have regarded themselves as better than everyone else. The worst example, I suppose, was Nazi Germany. Adolf Hitler convinced his people that they were a superior race. For the good of the world, they needed to exterminate inferior people like Jews, the handicapped, homosexuals, and other social misfits.

The Bible urges us not to think more highly of ourselves than we ought. We should honor others above ourselves (Romans 12:10). Humility is a virtue, while pride is a sin. It's certainly the root of many other sins. And yet, few of us sufficiently overcome pride.

I once contracted bronchitis and spent all day in bed. How could I get up and lead the Wednesday night Prayer Meeting? What could I do? About that time my fever spiked and I began hallucinating.

As my brain was barbequing, I saw a disturbing scene in heaven. Angels were standing around the throne of God, and everything seemed to be in bedlam. There was chaos in heaven! The angels were reading a news bulletin and were distraught. Then they passed it to Jesus. He took one look and cried out in alarm, "Oh no! What will we do? Pastor Curtis is sick, and it's Wednesday night!" Yes, it's just a fable, but it shows the madness—the hyperbole—of uncontrolled pride.

A newspaper reporter interviewed a famous businessman and asked him to what he attributed his success as a CEO. With a twinkle in his eye he explained, "It's been about fifty percent good employees, fifty percent good luck, and the rest is all brains."

> I'm proud to say that humility is one of my greatest assets!

Muhammad Ali, in his prime, was very full of himself, often proclaiming, "I am the Greatest!" As he embarked on an airplane, the flight attendant reminded him to fasten his seatbelt. Ali replied brashly, "Superman don't need no seatbelt." She shot back, "Superman don't need no airplane!" Sheepishly, Ali complied.

## PROUD MAN

**What was Naaman's greatness?** The General was the Syrian Army's Chief-of-Staff. He was a close advisor to the king, who saw him as a 'great man.' You might say he was the General Schwarzkopf of his day (or Grant, Eisenhower, Alexander the Great, or Marshall…).

God chose Naaman to bring judgment on His rebellious people, Israel. Consequently, Naaman became a great man throughout the region. But there was a blemish on Naaman's greatness. It was the incurable plague of that era—he had leprosy.

**Naaman had a hidden blessing.** A certain little Hebrew slave girl, captured on one of Naaman's raids into Israel, knew God's power. She was obscure by the standard of any era. But she cared about her master's wellbeing. She knew about the prophet Elisha. So, she told her Syrian mistress that Elisha could help with Naaman's leprosy. The woman passed the word to her husband, who quickly acted on the information.

Naaman made a journey to Israel, but he didn't know at the time that he was making a journey to humility.

**Naaman had a big ego.** To speculate about Naaman's ego is not strictly biblical. But put yourself in his shoes. Imagine what your ego might be like. This man was proud of his accomplishments, proud of his position, proud of his power, proud of his influence with the king. He was also conceited about his homeland and looked down on Israel and her muddy Jordan River.

Naaman knew how his healing should happen; it didn't involve the God of Israel. When God's prophet Elisha told him to dip himself in the Jordan River seven times, Naaman was uber–insulted. He might have snarled, "Don't you know who I am?" The Bible explains that Naaman went away in a rage!

In 1957 Christian Herter was running for reelection as governor of Massachusetts. One day, he arrived late at a campaign barbecue. He hadn't eaten all day, and he was famished. As he moved down the serving line, he held out his plate and received one piece of chicken.

The governor said to the serving lady, "Excuse me, do you mind if I get another piece of chicken? I am very hungry." The woman replied, "Sorry, I'm supposed to give one piece to each person." He repeated, "But I am starving." Again, she said, "Only one to a customer."

They say that Herter was normally a modest man. But he decided to throw his weight around a little. "Madam, do you know who I am? I am the governor."

"Mister," she replied, "do you know who I am? I'm the lady in charge of chicken—and I say one piece per person! Now move along, you're holding up the line." Herter subsequently retold the story with good humor.

## HUMBLED MAN

**Listen to a voice of reason.** Receiving good advice from subordinates can be difficult. "I'm the big shot here, not you. Why should I listen to your advice? In fact, who do you think you are, giving me advice?"

The servants of Naaman could see what he could not. "You would attempt some great feat if it would help you be healed," they reasoned with him. "Why not just try this little thing?" Thankfully, Naaman listened to the voice of reason. It made good sense. Trade pride for faith. Give God a chance to work through your humility and heal you.

**You can choose healing or haughtiness.** Naaman faced the choices we too face. "Will I accept God's healing on His terms? Or will I keep my pride and my sickness? Will I be humble and healed? Will I be proud and debilitated?"

At some point in life we should realize, like Naaman, "I have to get off the throne if I'm going to let God get on!" With Him on the throne of life, healing can happen. If I stubbornly refuse to vacate my throne—that might be how the problem first started! No single decision in all of life matters more than climbing down and surrendering to God as King of your life.

Most of us find the throne of life very comfortable. "It's my gilded chair; I can sit here if I want to!" even if it's just my worn out, ratty La–Z–Boy®. It's especially problematic if we've had success in some area of life. The achieving can dazzle us. Hopefully, there is someone to help us gain perspective.

TV personality Tom Brokaw was wandering through Bloomingdale's in New York City shortly after being promoted to co–host of the *Today Show*. It was a pinnacle for Brokaw after years of hard work in Omaha, then Atlanta, and finally for NBC in Los Angeles and Washington. Now, he anchored the famous *Today Show*. He was feeling good about himself. He spied a man in the store watching him closely. He kept staring. When he approached him, Brokaw was sure he was about to reap the first fruits of his newfound fame.

The man pointed his finger and said, "Tom Brokaw, right?" "Yes, that's right," said the rising star of NBC News.

"You used to do the TV news in Omaha, right?" "That's right," confirmed Brokaw.

"I knew it the minute I spotted you," the fellow said. Then he asked, "Whatever happened to you, anyway?"

## HEALED MAN

Naaman's pride had been blocking his recovery. The problem of the Prophet's instructions was not simply the humiliation of "seven ducks in muddy water." The obstacle was pride. Once he overcame it, healing could proceed.

**Less pride, more faith.** To embed this principle in my congregation's mind, I once had the west side of the sanctuary chant, "Less Pride!" while the east side responded, "More faith!" at the top of their lungs. There's life-changing truth in that formula.

The Syrian military commander decided to take a chance. He would trust this God of the Israelites. In order to trust Him, Naaman had to relinquish his anti-Semitic, big man on campus, Chairman of the Joint-Chiefs-of-Staff pride. When he humbled himself, there was room for faith to grow and healing to proceed. There was a direct correlation between Naaman's decreasing pride and his increasing faith. The same is always true for us, too.

## GRATEFUL MAN

Naaman's humility produced gratitude. His goal had been physical healing. It became a reality, thanks to God and His servant, Elisha.

Naaman offered gifts in gratitude for his healing, but to the wrong person. Elisha declined the rewards, knowing it was not he, but God, who had healed the General. Elisha wouldn't accept credit for something God had done. He too was humble.

**Humility and gratitude produced worship.** Naaman acknowledged that Israel's God, Who had healed him, was deserving of worship. It was his offering to God, the Healer. To demonstrate this he took soil from Israel on which to bow down, back in Syria, to the One True God.

His worship was a further act of humility. 'Everything Syrian' might be better than anything Israelite. But not the deity. He declared unending loyalty to Yahweh, saying he would never again worship the gods of Syria.

## HUMILITY HEALS

How many of us could be healed of whatever hurts so badly, but are too proud? How can our refusal of humility be worth the pain of our suffering? Many people live with their pain because they prefer it to humbly relinquishing their pride.

**Learn to live with pain and healing.** Swallowing pride is not a simple thing. It's not even easy to

### BTW

- **Gehazi** was the longtime servant to Elisha. He served faithfully, and once not so faithfully.

- He's mentioned seven times in 2 Kings chapter 4 regarding the Shunammite (see Chapter 12 of this book).

- He's mentioned seven more times in 2 Kings chapter 5, regarding the gifts Naaman offered Elisha after his healing. Gehazi tried to get a talent (75 lb.) of silver and two clothing outfits. He was outed by Elisha and was leperous from then on.

- Apparently it never occurred to him that Elisha, God's prophet, would see through Gehazi's duplicity.

- **THE LESSON:** *Secrets a person keeps from others are all known to God. The best way to guard against lies coming to the forefront is not to tell any. Make truth a nonnegotiable principle in life!*

recognize or define the pride that keeps a person in pain. My suffering is surely different from yours. Your pain differs from others.

However, the principles of healing are similar for each one. Naaman provides a great example of someone who had to travel on "Humble Highway" before he could be healed. One thing is sure: healing can happen when humility replaces pride!

**Accept your God-given humility.** You might recall that pride was the downfall of Satan. Being Archangel was not enough, he wanted to be god. And he's particularly skillful at producing pride in us. He is equally good at hiding our own pride from us.

We will never get over self-important arrogance until we sincerely ask God to root it out of our hearts and minds. The first and most critical step is to seek God's direction toward humility. The very first step on your journey to humility marks the beginning of healing from whatever afflicts you. As pride diminishes, faith in God can grow and ultimately result in recovery.

One concept that advances my pride-to-humility progress deals directly with my years of preaching and a Doctorate in Communication. I've taken to reminding myself, **"No one is as interested in what I have to say as I am!"** I also pray, "Lord, please teach me humility *without* humiliation!" Sometimes He says 'Yes!'

Pride blinds our eyes, stops our ears, ties our hands, hobbles our feet. When we give up our pride and learn humility, we can see and hear. We can touch the lives of others. **We can walk and run and move with purpose again. We can be made well and bless others.**

God requires humility before He's willing to heal us. Come to God humbly. Experience His healing as pride gives way to faith, and faith leads to a world of blessings.

## MOMENT OF TRUTH

As our pride diminishes, faith in God can grow and ultimately lead to a journey of healing and wellness.

**MY PERSONAL JOURNEY:** "Lord, please open my eyes and ears, loose my hands and feet. Show me if pride is keeping me from being effective for You." ☐ Yes ☐ No

- "God, please give me clear vision to see myself as those around me do. Here is how I can replace pride with godly humility":

  _____
  _____
  _____
  _____
  _____

- "If my pride decreases and my faith increases, I think I can be healed of the pain of":

  _____
  _____
  _____
  _____
  _____

# 16

# DEAL OR NO DEAL

### JOURNEY TO FULFILL GOD'S PLAN
— Hannah —
(1 Samuel 1:2–2:21)

### SPURGEON'S WELL

English Preacher, Charles Haddon Spurgeon, told of a deep well that had been dug at his home, some time before he owned the place. Spurgeon said that the owner was determined to strike water, no matter how deep the well had to go.

In those days, wells were dug by hand, using technology corresponding to the era. The well–diggers dug down a hundred feet, and found plenty of clay, then some mud, and then stone, but no water. Urged on by the owner, they went a second hundred feet, sending the earth and stones up out of the hole, bucket–by–bucket, on a rope. As they went further down, it grew darker and darker in the hole. In this stratum they found flint and thick, heavy sand, but still no water.

They wanted to quit, but their employer refused. And so, down into the third hundred feet they dug. By now they were understandably discouraged. But the man paying the bill would not be denied. Reluctantly they dug on in solid soil and gloomy near-darkness.

One day, lunchtime came, and still no water. So, the men left their tools at the bottom and winched upward the long, slow ascent and ate their cheerless meal, despondent at their lack of success. When they came back, fresh, clear water was gurgling into the hole, long-since drowning their digging tools. The clear water was rapidly filling the well.

The commitment of the owner was such that no expense was too great, no effort too much, to get the blessing of pure water.

A similar spirit lies at the core of our deepening relationship with God. He has the precious, life-giving water we want and need. He knows at what depth the water will spring into the well of our souls. Are we devoted enough to keep digging, to give whatever it takes to get what we need and want most from Him?

Hannah was that dedicated. She was so passionate for God's blessing that she was ready to give the most precious treasure she could think of. Hannah made a deal! God invites us to give Him the very best we have, the thing we cherish most in life. Can we trust Him that much? In Hannah's case, her response to God might have been…

## GIVE YOU WHAT? ANYTHING BUT THAT!

**Hannah was grieving.** Many couples experience heartache because they cannot have children. Kathy and I do not feel that pain for ourselves, though we comprehend the sadness of others. Kathy gave birth to our last child two months before she turned twenty-one. Our hearts have ached with others who were unable to have children. Often, human eyes can see what wonderful parents they would make.

Hannah was married to Elkanah, who had a second wife. She had several children and enjoyed rubbing Hannah's nose in her barrenness.

When the family made the annual journey to Shiloh, where God's tabernacle was, Elkanah always gave Hannah an extra portion of the good stuff, since he loved her so much. But it never eased her bitter grief.

Typical of men throughout history, Elkanah thought *he* was her prize. He asked her, "Aren't I worth more to you than ten sons?" Only Hannah's kindness kept her from screaming, "No, you are not! Don't be so full of yourself."

**Hannah lived life's worst tragedy.** In Hannah's day there was no misfortune worse than barrenness. The whole society viewed it as a curse directly from God. There was something wrong with you, or you were a terrible sinner, if you could not bear children. Not only did people look down on you, but it also opened the door to harassment.

Year after year Hannah made the journey to Shiloh, where God's house was located then. It was always a miserable experience. Her rival ridiculed her. What should have been a meaningful worship experience in the presence of God was made unbearable by the competitor who had children and used them to diminish Hannah.

**What was Hannah's treasure?** Nothing else in life meant more to Hannah than having a child. Without a baby, Hannah's life was miserable. It would get better only if she could bear Elkanah a son. It was probably the first thing she prayed about, and the last, every day of her existence.

She told Eli the High Priest that her life was deeply troubled and that she had "great anguish and grief." Despite a loving husband and a mostly–happy marriage, she was in despair. She was heartbroken. Bearing a child was the one treasure absent from her life.

**Hannah made an offer (Deal or No Deal?).** Bargaining with God is not something to do lightly. It's fraught with frustration, pitted with potholes. But Hannah was desperate. She cried out to God, "Lord God of heaven and earth, do You see my misery? Please don't forget about my anguish. If You will give me a son, I'll give him back to You. He would be my most cherished thing on earth. I will deliver him here to You. And I promise that he will al-

> **Some things in life are just too valuable to keep to yourself.**

ways live according to the vows I have made to You."

Sometimes, in our despair, we try to bargain with God. "Lord, if You will _____, then I will _____!" I don't recommend making deals with God. It often happens when we're distant from Him. We feel we have to make up for our unfaithfulness with improbable propositions. That clearly was not the case with Hannah. In her desperation, she looked for anything she could do to win God's favor. She was saying, "Lord if You will give me what I want most in all of life, I will give you my most prized possession—Oh wait! That would be the very thing I am asking from You."

Some things in life are simply too precious to keep to yourself. For Hannah, that precious thing was the life of her firstborn son. This was no idle, frivolous gift Hannah offered to God. This was a carefully-thought-out deal. "Lord, give me the best, most wonderful gift I could ever receive. In exchange, I will give it back to You!" Now, is that a deal or what?

It was a different bargain from all those I've ever tried to make with God. "Lord, give me {some material thing} I want, and I will read my Bible every day (and pray too, when I have the time)." "Lord, get me out of this mess I've gotten myself into, and I'll give a big offering to the building fund (well, not *that* big!)." "Lord, don't let me die on this airplane, and I'll go win all the lost people in China (1.4 billion!) for You!" "Lord, give me a million dollars, and I'll tithe ten percent back to You! Hey, make it fifteen percent! I'm feeling generous."

Using Hannah's pattern of bargaining with God, I would have to pray, "Lord, give me a million dollars and I'll give it all back to You—with interest!" Of course, He already owns it all!

**God rewarded Hannah.** The drama begins in 1 Samuel 1:19. The family went home from Shiloh and, in time, Hannah became pregnant. When her prized son was born, she named him Samuel (a rough equivalent of which is, "I have borrowed him from God.")

Hannah received the very thing she had pled for. When Samuel was weaned, it was "crunch time." Would she keep her part of the deal? Would she be able to give this precious son back to God?

When the time came, Hannah fulfilled her vow to the Lord and took Samuel to the Tabernacle of God. She kept her word and entrusted him into the care of the High Priest. From then on, his upbringing took place in a setting of devout service to God. He made good use of Samuel, who eventually earned the nickname, Israel's Seer (or Prophet).

**Hannah's reward was also her invoice.** God provided the "goods." Now, it was time for her to pay the bill. True to her word, Hannah journeyed with Samuel to God's house, and there she gave him to the Lord, as she promised.

This journey was different from all her other journeys to God's house at Shiloh. Hannah took her part of the bargain very seriously, as should we all, if we're so bold as to bargain with God. Pondering Hannah's deal with God and her faithful journey to complete the transaction, you should understand that God deserves and expects...

## ...NOTHING LESS THAN YOUR BEST!

**We face a predicament.** We are sinful and separated from God; we could never earn His goodwill in our lives. The essence of grace is God's generosity, even though we do not deserve it, nor can we earn it. We need God's favor and His blessings to empower and enrich us. We possess nothing that God needs, nothing with which to pay for His favorable treatment. And yet, He encourages us to make offerings to Him as a sign of our love and devotion. This is a king-sized predicament, indeed. If God welcomes our donations, what could we possibly give Him that would be a fitting offering?

**How precious to you is your treasure?** It doesn't matter exactly what it is. What really matters is how valuable the offering is to *you*! The God who owns everything in the universe doesn't care what you give to

Him. It's not like He needs anything you or I have. What He really cares about is How much does your offering to Him cost you? Is it really a sacrifice? Are you offering Him the very best you have, your most prized treasure? In trade for what you want, are you giving God something that you value highly?

## THE MANHATTAN PROJECT (1626, NOT 1945)

The Canarsie Delaware Indians didn't understand this principle of great value paid to complete a purchase. If they had known how little the Dutch merchants treasured the beads and trinkets, they wouldn't have sold Manhattan Island for the equivalent of twenty-four dollars. (Imagine selling all of Manhattan Island for today's equivalent of $887.26[39]) You see, any transaction of this kind must offer value to both sides. And when we seek something we value from God, we must give Him something of great value to us.

It's not about *what*, or *how much*, you offer to God—He already has it all. He has temporarily loaned it to you. It's really about **offering what is most precious to you!** Hannah understood that anything less was inadequate. God reciprocated—He turned around and blessed Hannah's life richly. Not only was there the love and joy she had in her relationship with Samuel. God blessed Hannah with a loving husband, Elkanah. And there were other children too—three sons and two daughters.

**Consider your challenge.** First, you must decide if God's blessings, His wonderful gifts of grace, are that important to you. "How badly do I want God to bless my life?"

Second, what can you offer Him as your gift of love, devotion and commitment? How highly do you treasure it? Will you even miss it when it's gone?

Finally, your challenge is to **step beyond the theoretical**. What will you *really do* as you make a deal—or no deal—with God? You can only

---
[39] https://www.officialdata.org/

step out in faith on the premise that *God only wants you!* And the most realistic way to give God *you* is to offer Him the things you prize and treasure most!

God asked Abraham to sacrifice the son of promise. But when dad took the step of obedience, God changed the plan. He gave Isaac back to his father. God's generosity will always outnumber yours.

## A REPAYMENT OF BLOOD, SWEAT AND TEARS

Arizona Senator and Vietnam Prisoner Of War John McCain told this story at the 1988 Republican National Convention in New Orleans: "In the final years of our imprisonment, the North Vietnamese moved us from small cells with one or two prisoners to large rooms with as many as thirty to forty men to a room. We preferred this situation for the companionship and strength we could draw from our fellow prisoners. Our captors also let us receive packages and letters from home. Many POWs received word from their families for the

### BTW

- **Samuel's** mother kept her promise and took Samuel to God's house. Eli became his guardian. God spoke to the little lad (see 1 Samuel 3).

- The first three times God called him by name, the boy ran to Eli, thinking he had heard the priest. The third time God spoke, Eli told him it was God's voice he was hearing.

- Finally Samuel knew God's voice, and answered, "Here I am. I'm listening!"

- **THE LESSON:** *If you want to know God's will in your life, you have to know Him well enough that you recognize His voice when He speaks.*

- Spend time with Him, share spiritual intimacy. When He speaks to You, you'll know it's Him and not the devil, a well meaning person, or even your own selfish whispers.

- You'd never ask a stranger his or her will for your life. So develop a close friendship with God; and know Him well.

first time in several years. The improved conditions were a result of public pressure put on the North Vietnamese by the American public.

"In our cell was one Navy officer, Lt. Commander Mike Christian. Over a period of time Mike had gathered bits and pieces of red and white cloth from various packages. Using a piece of bamboo he had fashioned into a needle, Mike sewed a crude United States flag on the inside of his shirt, one of the blue pajama tops we all wore.

"Every night in our cell, Mike would hang his shirt on the wall, and we would say the pledge of allegiance to the red, white and blue. I know that the pledge of allegiance may not be the most important aspect of our day now, but I can tell you that at the time it was the most important aspect of our lives.

"This had been going on for some time until one of the guards came in as we were reciting, 'I pledge allegiance to the flag, of the United States of America…' They ripped the flag off the wall and dragged Mike out. He was beaten for several hours and then thrown back into the cell.

"Later that night, as we were settling down to sleep on our concrete slab beds, I looked over to the spot where the guards had thrown Mike. There, under the solitary light bulb hanging from the ceiling, I saw him, still bloody and his face swollen beyond recognition. The brave man was gathering bits and pieces of cloth together. He was sewing a new American flag."[40]

If a man can have that depth of commitment to his flag and his country, how committed can you be to the Lord and Savior who died on the cross and rose from the grave to save you from eternal punishment?

---

[40] Fact Check: Story about a POW and flag he made is true (jacksonville.com)

> **MOMENT OF TRUTH**
>
> Give your highest quality, most prized gifts to God. He will pay them back, generously. You can never out–give God.

**MY PERSONAL JOURNEY:** Let me explain my situation (the need for this life journey):

_____
_____
_____
_____
_____

- The most precious treasure I have in life is:

_____
_____
_____
_____
_____

- Do I love God enough to give it to Him? ❑ Yes ❑ No ❑ I'm working on it

- In reality, how can I give this (or another priceless) treasure to God?

_____
_____
_____
_____
_____

# 17

# RETURN TO THE SCENE OF THE CRIME

**JOURNEY TO REPAIR A BROKEN PAST**
— Moses —
(Exodus 1–4)

**TASTES LIKE CROW**

On our first day in England, we flew from Dublin to Luton Airport and took a black London taxi into the great city. We found our way to the hotel and went across the street for lunch in a nice Italian café. We decided that, after we rode the double-decker "Big Bus," we'd come back for one of their rich European desserts.

Hours later, the bus dropped us off at Hyde Park. We walked across half the city of Westminster (really a fascinating experience, Old Chum) and returned to the restaurant for dessert. They refused to serve "just desserts." They were unmoved by our claim that we had eaten there at lunchtime. "We only serve full meals!" I was angry. It was stupid of them to refuse us dessert. I said a couple things I couldn't take back. Then I huffed my way out of the restaurant.

We walked down the block toward our hotel. Suddenly, I said, "Kathy, do you have the camera?" We frantically searched, but it was not with our stuff. She said, "We must have left it in that restaurant." Ooooh noooo!

I returned to the restaurant I had promised never to enter again, and asked the very same rude waiter if he had seen our camera since we left. "Even if he has, he won't give it to us" I thought. He was slightly more gracious than I anticipated, however. He handed it back with a smug little smirk reserved especially for rude, boorish Ami blokes.

I ate lunch in that restaurant, then tried unsuccessfully to eat dessert. Finally, I returned and **ate a generous serving of crow!**

Many people, maybe including you, have experienced events that produced anxiety, fear and even grief. Maybe your life is twisted by some cruel event in your past that has poisoned the present and threatens your future with failure, bitterness, regret, or lost opportunities.

One Bible character stands out when I think of lives twisted by lost opportunity: Moses. His life of great promise went south (actually *east*), and he had to make a journey, literally a "return to the scene of the crime," before his potential and his future could become what God intended.

Moses made three transformative life journeys: 1.) Flight from Egypt to avoid prosecution for murder. 2.) His return to face the music. 3.) When he led Israel out of Egypt home to Canaan. This chapter focuses on that journey back to Egypt to stand before Pharaoh. He faced the single event in his life that was holding his future hostage. Moses had to confront his painful past in order to experience God's promising future.

## MOSES'S JOURNEY, PAST, PRESENT AND FUTURE

**Moses had a dangerous birth and a surprising childhood.** He survived government genocide, the order to kill all Hebrew boys at birth. Thankfully, Moses's parents were "pro–life." Hiding him in a basket floating on the Nile River resulted in his adoption by a princess. God was guiding this journey.

What greater sign was there that God had a plan for this boy than his survival of government-sanctioned infanticide? Discovered by Pharaoh's daughter, she hired his own parents to raise him. Trained in the Hebrew faith and customs, he was legally the son of the Egyptian princess. He received the best education in the world (Egypt was arguably the most advanced, most powerful nation on earth at that time).

**Moses had a haunting past.** What squandered potential lay ahead: Pharaoh's adopted grandson, the best "Ivy League" education available, a position of influence on Capitol Hill. His desire to help his own oppressed people, however, turned things ugly.

Moses went out among the people and observed firsthand the mistreatment of the Hebrews. His upbringing in a Hebrew home certainly influenced his sympathies. His overzealous effort to stop the abuse resulted in the murder of an Egyptian guard. Realizing that his crime was known, he escaped to Midian in Sinai, just one step ahead of the law, as they say.

Back in Egypt, there were people who wanted to bring this interloper to justice. All hopes for power and glory, all that potential for good, all wasted. It was more than just his "Wanted Dead or Alive" status—it was all the lost prospects, the dashed hopes, the dreams of what could have been, "if only..." All his dreamed-of accomplishments were short-circuited by one fatal mistake.

**A bleak, dead-end present dulled the soul.** As we find Moses facing God in Exodus chapter three, he was finishing forty years as a lowly shepherd, taking the sheep to pasture on "the far side of the desert." You can't get much more remote than that. The Grandson of Pharaoh, who was highly trained, from the respected tribe of Levi, had spent those forty years herding stupid, smelly, stubborn sheep. Probably missed the funerals of both his parents. He lived half his life separated from sister Miriam and older brother Aaron.

> It's a calamity when someone's future is held hostage by a cursed, tragic past.

As we learn later in Exodus, those sheep were a good preparation for leading the headstrong Israelites. His father-in-law Jethro was Priest of the Lord in Midian, yet Moses was doing the lowliest chores. He was eighty years old by this time, still at an entry-level point in his sheepherding career, working for his father-in-law. Talk about a dead-end job!

His bleak, bottom-man-on-the-totem-pole *present* made his *future* seem even more hopeless. Perhaps he forgot his dreams of accomplishing great things. But God broke into Moses's humdrum, dead-end life. He had already forgiven him of his sins. Had Moses forgiven himself?

God was about to take him out of his bleak life. But curiously, He had to talk Moses into it first. If his past crime was not holding him hostage, at least in his mind, why would he resist this great new opportunity God offered? A bush was burning but not consumed. Moses's curiosity got the better of him. He went to look and was confronted by God in life-changing ways. The historical encounter assumed epic proportions.

**A light flickered in the tunnel.** God made him an offer from the burning bush he could hardly refuse. But Moses was full of excuses:

- He said to God, "Who am I, that I should go to Pharaoh and bring the Israelites out of Egypt?" (Exodus 3:11).
- When God told him to go back to his suffering people in Egypt, Moses answered, "What if they do not believe me or listen to me and say, 'The Lord did not appear to you'?" (4:1).
- Moses said to the incendiary bush, "O Lord, I have never been eloquent, neither in the past nor since you have spoken to your servant. I am slow of speech and tongue." (4:10).

- When he finally ran out of excuses, Moses lamely fell back on "O Lord, please send someone else to do it" (4:13).

Why was Moses so reluctant to go? Was it poor self-esteem? Was it fear of rejection? Was it fear of speaking in public? Did Moses love his ho-hum life so much that he could not bear to give it up? All those things may have been factors in his reluctance. But probably they were smokescreens for the real issue.

One of the primary reasons Moses did not want to go back to Egypt was the cloud under which he left, the accumulated cumulus of his past. When he ran away from Egypt, there was a death sentence over his head (Exodus 4:19). Forty years later, Moses's past still held him hostage. He was a brilliant, talented, educated man, herding sheep for his father-in-law on the back side of Sinai.

The flip side was that this opportunity to lead the Hebrews out of bondage and back to Israel was a dream come true for Moses!

### BTW

- **Moses's Followers** were the bane of his existence. They were stubborn, lacked vision and sometimes trusted Egypt's gods more than God Himself.

- The Israelites complained constantly about water, food, Moses's leadership style, how much better they thought it had been in Egypt, yada yada yada.

- Once, God told Moses He was going to destroy the people and raise up a new nation with Moses as the patriarch.

- In his humility (Moses was called the most humble man on the face of the earth; Numbers 12:3), he asked God to destroy him with the people. God relented and preserved Israel.

- Over and over God showed His loving patience with the people, though from time to time He had to discipline them.

- **THE LESSON:** *There's not always joy in leadership. Hard decisions are integral to leading. Some see only glory and power, but leadership demands toughness, vision for the future and placing your followers ahead of yourself.*

Here's how Hebrews 11:24–26 explains it: "By faith Moses, when he had grown up, refused to be known as the son of Pharaoh's daughter. He chose to be mistreated along with the people of God rather than to enjoy the pleasures of sin for a short time. He regarded disgrace for the sake of Christ as of greater value than the treasures of Egypt, because he was looking ahead to his reward."

The future offered both ominous risks and exciting prospects. Have you ever experienced that? Wavering between dread and delight? His was a future that could not happen unless Moses "returned to the scene of the crime" and faced the event that gripped his past, handcuffed his present, and eclipsed his future.

## MOSES'S "HAPPY ENDING"

**God handled the objections.** This conversation in Exodus 3:4–4:17 reminds me of what they teach salespeople. "All the buyer's objections are just requests for 'permission to buy!'" "Don't let them down; give your permission to make the purchase!" "Don't take 'no' for an answer. The buyer needs your help!" God handled each of Moses's objections, one-by-one.

Part of Moses's dilemma was that he couldn't just 'sneak in the back door.' He had to stand before Pharaoh. True, it was a different Pharaoh than his grandfather. But he held life-and-death power in the most dominant nation on earth.

Finally, after their rumble in the desert, Moses gave in to God's continued persuasion and agreed to go back. He decided to make the unpleasant journey and confront his past. He would deal with it and move into God's preferred future. It was (gulp) confirmed.

**Moses faced the king.** It all happened just as God had promised. Moses and his brother Aaron brought together all the elders of Israel and explained God's instructions. God validated it with miracles. When the people heard that God had not forgotten them, they bowed down in worship. Afterward, the brothers went to Pharaoh and told him what God required.

Pharaoh's reaction was predictable. "Who is this Lord of yours, that I should obey him and let your people go? I do not know the Lord and I will not let Israel go." With the help of God, Moses was able to stand before the most powerful man on earth and deliver the word of the Lord. God was perhaps the only power on earth greater than Pharaoh!

Moses wasn't arrested for his crime. In fact, it doesn't seem to have come up at all. Which underscores a common truth: Often, our fearful "What ifs" are not as bad as we think they will be. Often, they're powerless over us even though we run from them.

The enemy uses fear, confusion, frustration and intimidation to keep us bound in our failed, unproductive present because of a sin or mistake from our distant past—usually one that, in reality, is far less devastating than it is in our imaginations.

The enemy knows that the past doesn't have the power to bind us unless we empower it. Even when the consequences are serious, we can break the chains of our past and be freed of its power. A cnn.com article in 2004 reported that Dan Leach dealt with his sinful past, and in so doing, had to suffer the consequences. After watching the Mel Gibson movie, *The Passion of the Christ*, the twenty-one-year-old Texan confessed to killing his ex-girlfriend. He rigged the murder to look like a suicide. In fact, the investigators concluded it really was suicide. Leach was off scot-free. But after seeing Mel Gibson's powerful movie about Jesus's crucifixion, Leach came forward and confessed. He was then sentenced to seventy-five years in prison for the grisly act.

With God's help, Moses confronted his past and allowed God to break the shackles that bound his freedom! You might say Moses did a sentence of forty years of exile "on the back side of the desert" for his crime!

**Moses's life became productive.** Forty years in Egyptian preparation for a productive life led to forty years as a 'rank–and–file–shepherd' in the desert, because of the murder he committed. In Sinai, Moses had no prospects of advancement and no productive service to God. His past locked him into the bleak present he was enduring. But once Moses confronted his past, he was liberated to pursue the wonderful opportunities God prepared for him.

Through a series of powerful acts, God pried Pharaoh's fingers from around the chosen people. After ten dynamic demonstrations of God's superiority over Egypt's gods, Israel's liberation became a reality. It only happened when Moses willingly journeyed back to the scene of the crime and confronted his haunting past. I'm not so sure "happy ending" best describes Moses's forty years leading the Israelites. In fact, Scripture reveals a man known to complain bitterly about his burden, the people of Israel. But his life counted for eternity. "Productive" is a better description of Moses's influence on the rest of world history. All because he was reluctantly willing to confront his painful past and face the music.

## YOUR PAST, PRESENT AND FUTURE

**Start with your birth and growing up years.** Few of us had the privileges and opportunities Moses had. Are you the adopted son or daughter of a princess? Do you sport an Ivy League education? Maybe not. Of course, few of us were under such a cloud of infanticide as Moses either. You may feel that the cloud you're under is from your birth or upbringing. Not that you had control over either of those. But everyone is shaped by the past.

**A counterproductive present may be a prelude to a bright future in Christ.** Most of us have things in our pasts of which we're ashamed, or worse. In many cases, those circumstances are not as damaging as we have let them become. For all his trepidation, Moses's crime of passion was no obstacle when God paved the road ahead.

The truth remains, however, that many are tied in knots by their birth and upbringing or by some past event. You may be living a debilitating present because of those past events. Maybe life is ho–hum, gray and bleak, or dead–end. Many people trace their unsatisfying present to past errors or sins, to faulty choices or decisions.

Like Moses, we cannot confront the monsters in our past by ourselves. We need God's help. Only a fool insists on confronting past pain and problems without the divine guidance God offers. Some think, "I have to clean myself up before I can come to God." To you, I say, "You couldn't possibly clean yourself up enough to be okay with God." That's the domain of grace. Some say, "I got myself into this mess. I'll get myself out." Sorry, that's a pipe dream.

There are those who believe, "I don't want to be obligated to God; He'll probably ask me to do something I don't want to do." Only God can permanently and positively handle the baggage in our lives. There are inflamed issues that stymie our present and postpone our God–given future. There is simply nowhere else to turn. God has a bright and positive future in mind for you, no matter what your past and present are like. Do not let an unhappy, painful past derail your God–given future.

**Trust me, I'm your father.** Mike Huckabee former governor of Arkansas, says, "When John Mark was four years old, he was out playing in the back yard and got a splinter in his foot. He came in and held up his foot. He was crying, and…'I said, 'Sit on the couch. Let's take a look at it.'

"Then, as he held up his foot and I reached over to pull the splinter out (because I knew it would feel better), he said what every kid says: 'Don't touch it.' I said…I've got to touch it, Son…There is no choice.' 'It will hurt,' he moaned. I said, 'It might, but it won't hurt as long. It will sure feel a lot better when I get the splinter out.'

"But somehow, that was not adequate. So, Janet held down the top of him while I tried to hold down the bottom of him and pull that splinter out. He was kicking and screaming and jerking in all different directions...

"I wanted to say to him, 'Son, don't you trust me? What do you think I'm going to do, cut your foot off? I'm not here to hurt you. I'm here to help you, and if you won't let me help you, it's going to get worse, not better. Trust me; I'm your father. I love you. I care about you. I do this only to help you. Be still. Relax."[41]

A painful past can be like that. Until Dad fixes it, healing will not happen. Until the offending piece is removed, it will continue to hurt. Only when you've gone to God and let Him pull that splinter will you have relief. Sometimes, the fixing is painful (just ask the guy who confessed to murder after seeing *The Passion of the Christ*). Making that journey will allow you to get right with God, heal the scars of your past, remove the infection in your present, and tone the spiritual muscles as you move forward into your God–given future.

---

**MOMENT OF TRUTH**

With God's help, we can make our journey back to "the scene of the crime." When we confront our past, we can make peace with ourselves, others and God. And we can move forward into our God–given future.

---

**MY PERSONAL JOURNEY:** My present ranks about here:

0   1   2   3   4   5   6   7   8   9   10

Totally un-satisfactory        Mixed bag        Totally satisfactory

---

[41] Preaching Today, Tape No. 78

- An event or action from my past that is poisoning my present is:

  _____
  _____
  _____
  _____
  _____

- This story of Moses's journey to wholeness inspires me in this way:

  _____
  _____
  _____
  _____
  _____

- If I could just do this, my future would be much better:

  _____
  _____
  _____
  _____
  _____

- Prayer: "Lord, please help me deal with this situation from my past. It has negatively affected my present life, and I know it is limiting my God-given future. With Your help, I will pacify my painful past and become all You want in my future. Amen!"

# 18

# THE LONG AND WINDING ROAD

### JOURNEY TO LEARNING AND WISDOM
— Queen of Sheba —
(1 Kings 4:29–34; 10:1–13; 2 Chronicles 9:1–12)

## JOURNEY TO WISDOM

Some journeys defy clear descriptions. We may embark on a journey we don't understand, like Abraham, or endure things we cannot explain, like Joseph. Philip the Evangelist didn't know the details of his journey, but he willingly obeyed, and God spread His Good News through him. We might make a journey because we're tied by an unlikely but unbreakable love to someone else, as Ruth did.

Other journeys are crystal clear. Moses knew well his criminal past and that he had to confront it before he could accept God's ultimate challenge. David perceived what lay ahead. It was just a matter of refusing to settle for second-best. Abigail could envision slaughter if she refused God's journey to make peace.

In this chapter, we travel alongside a little-known woman whose passion for wisdom and knowledge pushed her out the door to journey on the long, harsh road to Jerusalem. Whether Sheba was in southern

Arabia or even farther in the southwest region of Ethiopia, the endeavor was lengthy, uncomfortable and expensive. And yes, it was risky.

> **I now know that I don't know almost everything.**

King Solomon's wisdom was world-famous and this woman had many questions burning in her mind. So, the Queen of Sheba set out, traveling an arid, rutted, parched road she believed would take her to the fertile mind of the world's wisest man. Ah, the quest was wisdom!

When Kathy and I visited England, we traveled with our missionary daughter to Oxford, the home of perhaps the world's most famous university (a collection of forty-plus individual colleges). We saw famous colleges, like Magdalen (where CS Lewis taught), Trinity and Christ Church College. We also encountered lesser-known ones, like Brasenose and Oriel. Then there was Lincoln College, founded more than sixty years before Columbus discovered America. John Wesley, the future founder of worldwide Methodism, served for a time as lecturer and class moderator there.

Wesley once said, "When I was young, I was sure of everything; in a few years, having been mistaken a thousand times, I was not half so sure of most things as I was before; at present, I am hardly sure of anything but what God has revealed to me."[42] Someone else explained, "When I was seventeen, my father was totally stupid. By the time I reached twenty-five, it was amazing how much the old man had wised up!"

This attitude is common. I vaguely remember a time when there was hardly anything I did not know. Later, however, I found out that there were many things I didn't know. **Today, I know that I don't know almost everything**.

Will Rogers, that Oklahoma sage, once explained, "Everybody is ignorant, only on different subjects." Vern McLellan said, "He who thinks

---

[42] Evelyn Bence (Compiler), New Beginnings: Celebrate the Fresh Starts of Life. Old Tappan: Fleming H. Revell, 1988

education is costly should try ignorance." And Billy Graham pinpointed what the Queen of Sheba was about to learn. **"Knowledge is horizontal. Wisdom is vertical—it comes down from above."**

English preacher Charles Spurgeon put a philosophical spin on it when he said, "Wisdom is the right use of knowledge. To know is not to be wise. Many men know a great deal and are all the greater fools for it. To know how to use knowledge is to have wisdom."

The quest for biblical understanding may require a lifelong journey. It's worth every step. All who accept this venture receive far more than the trip costs them.

What follows is a fascinating story about one woman's quest for wisdom and knowledge and God's response to her journey.

## THE QUEEN HAD A PASSION

This passion for wisdom, insight and understanding is the most believable explanation for the Queen of Sheba's taxing journey. She made the long trek with a huge retinue. All the valuables she brought as gifts to Solomon indicate the importance she attached to her journey. Coincidentally, the biblical writer, Solomon, assigned feminine pronouns to wisdom.

**Solomon's wisdom was famous throughout the known world.** His great insight was given directly by God. He was wiser than the great seers of the East and of Egypt. Even far away, Solomon's reputation was known. "His fame spread to all the surrounding nations."

The Queen of Sheba had hard questions to discuss. She came to the right person for answers. Solomon's God-given insight fielded some tough challenges that day, and according to Scripture, he was equal to the task.

In his lifetime, Solomon wrote three thousand proverbs expressing life truths. He composed over one thousand songs. He codified plants, animals and birds, even reptiles and fish (1 Kings chapter 4). Call it an update on Adam's good work in Eden. The kings of the known world sent their ambassadors to learn what the King of Israel knew.

What questions would you like answered? Here are three good ones:

- *First,* how can a tiny, helpless, innocent baby melt the hearts of linebackers, lumberjacks and longshoremen?
- *Second,* how can Earth appear to be so old, when Genesis, and a large array of discoveries, age it at about six thousand years?
- *Third,* why does God let terrible things like tsunamis, terrorist attacks and child abuse continue?

The Bible suggests the Queen was a woman who thought deeply, with great intellectual curiosity. She actively sought answers to profound mysteries. This opportunity to discuss "all she had on her mind" was a once–in–a–lifetime chance. Imagine being able to go to one person who could answer every question imaginable (such a wise person might be nicknamed Encyclopedia Britannica®). That's a worthwhile journey, no matter where you might have to go.

### BTW

- **Human wisdom vs. God's.** How often does history reveal people who think they know better than God what they should do?
- The many examples of the failures of human thinking defy enumeration.
- Suffice it to say that a main theme in history is the elevation of humankind's thinking above the Word of God.
- 1 Corinthians chapter 1 is packed full of what God thinks of this egregious human error.
- **THE LESSON:** *Perhaps Proverbs 14:12 is the best expression of God's view: "There is a way that seems right to a person, but in the end, it leads to death."*
- Whenever you think of doing your own thing instead of what the Bible says, quote this verse to yourself. Let it remind you that God's way is always, always, always better than human wisdom.

The quest for knowledge and wisdom has led many people on extended journeys. Some of them never returned. The quest was more important than life itself.

## THE QUEEN'S PASSION LED TO ACTION

Passion without action is worthless. Here's a true story that comes from the sinking of the Titanic. You may have a passion for preserving your own life—most do.

Charles Swindoll told of a frightened woman (fear can be *passionate*) who sat in a lifeboat waiting to be lowered into the frigid North Atlantic. She suddenly remembered something she desperately needed and asked permission to return to her stateroom before they cast off (Passion can lead to *action*). They gave her three minutes, or they would leave without her.

She scrambled across the deck, already slanted precariously. She raced through the casino, ankle–deep cash rolling to one side. At her stateroom she frantically pushed aside her expensive jewelry, reaching to the shelf above her bed for three small oranges. She hurried back to the lifeboat and got in.

It seems ludicrous, because a short time earlier she wouldn't have chosen an entire grove of oranges over even the smallest diamond she owned. But death stalked the Titanic. One blast of its frigid breath had altered her values. Suddenly, the invaluable became insignificant. Worthless things were now beyond priceless. In that moment she treasured three oranges over a crate of diamonds. Passion led to action, which led to reward—food for the terrifying night at sea. (Swindoll's Ultimate Book of Illustrations & Quotes)

**Solomon answered "all her questions."** As hard as it is to imagine, "...nothing was too hard for him to explain to her" (2 Chronicles 9:2). Such is God–given wisdom. Combined with faith in God, it can satisfy any quest.

Don't miss the principle at the heart of the matter: "The quest requires the *journey!*" Are you willing to make such wisdom and knowledge your life's quest? Could it be the razor-sharp focus of your lifelong journey into insight? The Queen's passion led her to act. Her action produced a great reward. No wishful thinking here! Let's *do* something about it.

## THE QUEEN'S ACTION LED TO REWARD

**The Queen was overwhelmed.** Wisdom can be like that. Even a cynical, hardened person may be overwhelmed by the profound nature of God, the source of all knowledge. Solomon's insights, given by none other than God Himself, far exceeded the Queen's expectations. Sometimes we expect profound but instead get useless drivel. Other times we expect very little and get wisdom founded in God.

Swiss theologian Karl Barth traveled to America on a speaking tour in 1962. A reporter asked him, "Dr. Barth, what is the most profound thing you have ever heard?"

Barth sat pondering the question, smoke from his pipe circling overhead. Then he smiled and said, in his halting Swiss accent, "Jesus loves me, this I know, for the Bible tells me so." The wisdom of Solomon was deep for the simple fact that its source was God, not man.

**The Queen praised God.** The people of Sheba were Semitic (the same ancient bloodline as Jews and Arabs). The Sabeans (if that's what she was) were not known as followers of Israel's God. Still, in the presence of such godly insight, the Queen broke out in a song of admiration. "Praise be to the LORD your God, who has delighted in you and placed you on the throne of Israel. Because of the Lord's eternal love for Israel, he has made you king to maintain justice and righteousness" (1 Kings 10:9). Such obvious godly wisdom could elevate anyone to praise and worship, bowing in the presence of Him who created the universe by the word of His mouth.

**The Queen discovered the justice and righteousness of God.** Her journey of discovery showed her the clear truth that God cares deeply about justice and righteousness. For any mistreated, oppressed person, justice is a fond hope, though often unrealized. Biblical wisdom reveals God's care for mistreated, oppressed people. He is concerned about justice, though not always as swift to deliver as you might prefer.

Furthermore, God is deeply committed to righteousness, defined as "Right living according to God's Word!" No worldview that ignores justice and righteousness can be considered godly, biblical or wise.

**The Queen got more than she spent.** What a profound truth this brief story of the Queen of Sheba's long journey reveals. "King Solomon...gave her more than she had brought to him" (2 Chronicles 9:12).

She didn't set out on this lengthy journey, spend a fortune, endure hardship, boredom, aches and pains, and of course, danger, to profit monetarily. She undertook this quest so she could ponder the wisdom of God. She took home even more than she brought with her. The Scripture can have a double meaning: more wealth than she gave to Solomon. But also more wisdom than she brought, more than she ever thought possible.

## PASSION LEADS TO ACTION LEADS TO REWARD

**Prerequisite—a passion for Scripture.** Virtually everyone has a passion for living pain-free, successful, well-adjusted lives. Who wouldn't want to have a source that helps them make satisfying, productive decisions that contribute to the good life?

Many have a passing interest in the Bible. Often their interest is insufficient to actively pursue biblical insight and understanding. Only a genuine, enduring passion for wisdom from God's self-revelation, the Bible, will actually prompt a lifelong journey to cultivate godly wisdom.

**Journey to the biblical pot-of-gold.** Do you have a passion for biblical truth that results in action? Or does an "inactive" attitude describe your passion? Does it interest you, but not enough to mine the Scriptures for their nuggets of insight?

The Bible equates the quest for insight and understanding to mental, emotional and spiritual nourishment. The promises are many to all who embrace this challenge. Find a sampling of what Solomon wrote about wisdom at the end of this chapter.

**Reap the rewards of the journey to gain biblical understanding.** Just as the Queen of Sheba reaped profits beyond anything she spent, your journey to godly insight and experience will reward you, too. As your expedition takes you through the Bible, you'll discover God in ways you've never known Him before. You'll encounter self-awareness you never could obtain any other way. You'll excavate resources to enhance harmonious relationships, divine and human. You'll apply truths of a successful, satisfying, purpose-filled life you cannot acquire elsewhere.

**Memorize the first law of profit-making:** *With God, you always get more than you give!* This is a simple but profound reality, true even more so in the spiritual realm. The quest for wisdom pays a big bonus. However much you spend on your journey, you'll get more than you give.

In the words of twelfth-century cleric, Bernard of Clairvaux, "There are those who seek knowledge for the sake of knowledge; that is Curiosity. There are those who seek knowledge to be known by others; that is Vanity. There are those who seek knowledge in order to serve; that is Love."[43]

---

**MOMENT OF TRUTH**

A passion for biblical wisdom and insight demands a lifetime journey. It will be worth every expense, every hardship, every demand.

---

**MY PERSONAL JOURNEY:** Read through the wisdom of Solomon (Psalms 72 and 127, Proverbs, Ecclesiastes and Song of Solomon). Read one

---

[43] Bernard of Clairvaux Quotes (Author of On Loving God (Volume 13) | Good-reads

chapter a day (There are 51 chapters, total, in these four books). Read Monday through Friday and finish in ten weeks.

- Search what the Bible has to say about *'wisdom,' insight* and *'knowledge'* (use a concordance, reference books, commentaries, trustworthy online resources). Here are my findings:

_____

_____

_____

_____

_____

- Head out on your own biblical journey of discovery. Read through the Bible (The American Bible Society®, YouVersion®, OneYearBibleOnline.com and others all publish guides).

- Check it out: are you receiving more than you are spending in this quest?

_____

_____

_____

_____

_____

- A small sampling of what Solomon wrote about wisdom in Proverbs:
- 2:1–6, 10–12 • 4:5–7 • 8:10–11 • 9:10 • 16:16 • 23:23 • 24:14

# 19

# ROAD TO REDEMPTION

**JOURNEY TO REDEEM THE CULTURE**
— The Daniel Model —
(Daniel 1:1–21)

### FOREVER FOOTPRINTS

Canada has a national park on Ellesmere Island, the northernmost point in North America. It sits just four hundred eighty miles across the icecap from the North Pole. Ellesmere Island Park is very controversial. The permafrost there is so fragile that a careless footprint can last for decades. Longfellow wrote in *A Psalm of Life*:

> Lives of great men all remind us, we can make our lives sublime.
> And, departing, leave behind us footprints in the sands of time.[44]

    A visitor to Ellesmere truly leaves footprints that live on. In a larger sense, we all engage in journeys of influence that survive the test of time. Everyone leaves footprints that stamp good or bad on others, often for a lifetime. Some leave footprints that last for centuries. Very few leave footprints that endure forever. Like Jesus!

---

[44] . A Psalm of Life by Henry Wadsworth Longfellow | Poetry Foundation • www.poetryfoundation.org/poems/44644/a-psalm-of-life

Think about how you influence your culture with the values you embrace. Scott Adams created the Dilbert cartoon strip in two thousand newspapers in twenty-five languages. He wrote, "You don't have to be a 'person of influence' to be influential. In fact, the most influential people in my life are probably not even aware of the things they've taught me."[45]

In this chapter, we examine three Bible characters who took different paths that influenced their surrounding cultures. Jonah was hostile to the culture. Esther perpetuated the predominating cultural values of her time and place. (On a positive note, she saved her people.) And Daniel took a redemptive journey, from Israel to Babylon, to influencing the societies in which he was forced to live. Which of these is the surest way to influence the world for Jesus Christ?

## JONAH'S WAY: GIVE 'EM HELL!

**Jonah hated the anti-Israel Culture.** God specifically sent Jonah to Nineveh, the capital of Assyria, to preach salvation. God's purpose was to rescue the great pagan city from divine destruction. Assyria had taken captive the people of the ten northern tribes of Israel. The Jews hated them, as many Americans hated the Soviet Union immediately after World War II. The war, the land grab of Eastern Europe, and the nuclear threat were still raw, open sores on our nation's collective psyche.

Jonah's attitude toward God's call to love and serve the wicked Assyrians was clear. He hated them and refused to try rehabilitating the brutal world power of the eighth century B.C.

Jonah wanted revenge, not redemption. He resisted God's show of mercy, withholding the judgment they deserved. Like most of his fellow-Jews, Jonah wanted them all dead, not saved by God's grace. He so resented God's call to help that he jumped on a ship going west across the Mediterranean instead of overland east to Nineveh (modern-day Mosul, Iraq). He wanted the very worst imaginable fate for the godless

---

[45] https://deepstash.com/idea/202066/you-dont-have-to-be

Assyrians.

**Jonah was antagonistic to the culture.** It's easy to see why Jonah resisted influencing his enemies for good. His desire was contrary to God's. He wanted the Assyrian culture to crumble; God wanted it redeemed.

How often have you read the news and hoped God would nuke the evil culture around you? "Come on, God. Punish those wicked people who seem intent on trampling You in the mud. They oppose believers trying to redeem the culture."

I ruefully admit that I have begged the Lord of grace and mercy, "Forget mercy and grace; give 'em justice! (Dare I say it, "Give 'em hell!") God wants mercy, blessing and forgiveness for my cultural enemies. I'm passionate about revenge and punishment; and a pox on their blighted souls. I would ignore George Eliot's "Blessed is the influence of one true, loving human soul on another." I'd be out for blood!

If I chose Jonah's approach to cultural influence, I would resist the greatest power for good—God's love for sinners. Win the Africans, Asians and South Americans to faith in Jesus Christ if you must. But eradicate those whose selfish, godless ideas threaten this land I love.

## ESTHER'S WAY: STAY INVISIBLE

**Esther was hand-in-glove with the culture.** Before the rise of Haman's antisemitic threat to destroy all Jews in the Persian Empire, a secret Jew came to the throne as Queen. Her given name was Hadassah, but she was known to King Xerxes's court by her royal name, Esther. She was an orphan raised by her cousin, a Jewish employee of the state named Mordecai. Her connection to him was unknown until later.

The back story involved the insubordinate Queen Vashti, who refused to parade herself before the King's guests during a state celebration. We don't know for sure, but the King may have been offering his dinner party a pornographic floor show, and Vashti refused to comply—good for her. The result was her removal and a "Persian–style American Idol" search for a more compliant Queen. Esther was crowned and took her place beside her husband on the throne. She was no doubt breathtakingly beautiful. The King enjoyed her poise and cultured ways.

Esther fit into the prevailing culture of Persia like a pampered hand in a calfskin glove. For example, Esther was a member of Xerxes's harem during the selection process. All the usual practices of a typical harem were no doubt engaged.

She worked hard to blend with the cultural norms and mores of her adopted land. Persia was an idolatrous society steeped in materialism and pleasure–seeking hedonism. The values it held and promoted were very different from Israelite culture. The Jewish people had been deported from Israel at least a century before Esther's rise to prominence. In fact, their intentional aloofness from the cultures around them is a key factor in the many bloody purges of God's cho-

### BTW

- **DANIEL,** the honest, trustworthy Hebrew, lived his challenging life with integrity and godly character.

- He served 5 different kings (how often does a political appointee survive even one presidential change?)

- Deported to Babylon by Nebuchadnezzar, Daniel also served his succcessors, Evil–merodach and Belshazzar. When the Medes and Persians conquered Babylon, Daniel served Cyrus and his successor, Darius.

- In fact, not only was he a valued leader in government, at least Darius had a strong affection for him. Daniel, trapped in the lions' den, benefited from a father–son relationship with Darius.

- Daniel served the pagan "enemy" with integrity, faithfulness, even godliness.

- **THE LESSON:** *Remain God's man or woman, no matter what the circumstances. God will reward you.*

sen people throughout the millennia.

**Esther was content to perpetuate the culture.** Before Prime Minister Haman threatened the very survival of the Jewish people in Persia, Esther chose the path of least resistance. She adopted Persian ways that accommodated an easy, comfortable lifestyle. She found many reasons not to rock the cultural boat. In fact, Esther must have scrupulously avoided even a ripple of controversy. It was Vashti's agitating that got her deposed. Esther was careful to keep the status quo.

Even during the "Miss Persia" beauty pageant, she failed to mention her nationality. It was an intended oversight aimed to win her a coveted and favored position within the government and culture of Persia. Some would call it "situational ethics."

**The Queen was fearful of not fitting in.** Esther surely understood that she needed to blend in, not put her differences on display, if she was to succeed as the new national queen. When her father–figure cousin, Mordecai, came to her with news that all the Jews were to be killed, ironically by the king's edict influenced by the evil Haman, she was afraid to approach Xerxes to admit her Jewishness and seek his help.

Mordecai reminded her that she would not be safe in the palace even while all other Israelites were being exterminated. He urged her to take a stand against this culture of death provoked by antisemitic prejudice.

Mordecai highlighted the obvious: "You've arisen to the queenship for this very moment. If you refuse to help, God will provide deliverance from another source, but you will pay the price for your weakness."

Notice that when confronted with this terrifying reality, Esther changed course, no longer seeking to hide out in the palace. Instead, she spoke up, ultimately saving the Jews of Persia.

The Queen's position made her cultural activism amenable to Xerxes. She influenced him to amend the law so that Jews could protect themselves. This effectively turned the tables on those who would attack Esther's people. As Ken Blanchard explains, "The key to successful leadership is influence, not authority."[46] So it proved in fifth-century B.C. Persia.

## DANIEL'S WAY: INTEGRITY

In the year 606 B.C., Babylon took some of the best Israeli youths into exile, including Daniel, Hananiah, Mishael and Azariah. Nine years later, Babylon plundered Jerusalem. Finally, Babylon destroyed the Jewish temple in 587 B.C. For Daniel and his Hebrew fellow-exiles, the long, dusty road eastward across the Iraqi desert paved the way for his journey to influence the pagan culture.

A member of the Jewish royal family, Daniel stood head and shoulders above the rest. He was a physical specimen with great mental aptitude. In fact, when the King tested him, Daniel and his three friends were "ten times better" than the Babylonian intellectuals (Daniel 1:20).

Part of Daniel's orientation into Babylonian society was a three-year training and lifestyle regimen, including meals of food prepared for the King himself. This menu was a far cry from the kosher foods prescribed by the Jewish Law. "But Daniel resolved not to defile himself with the royal food and wine" (Daniel 1:8). He didn't rant in hatred against the culture in which he found himself, like Jonah. Neither did he conform to what was contrary to God's best life, as Esther did at first.

Daniel proposed a compromise. He and his three Jewish companions preferred to eat nothing but vegetables and drink water. When the King's steward feared the four men would look washed out and he would be blamed, Daniel proposed a brief trial. At the end of the test, Daniel, Shadrach, Meshach and Abednego "looked healthier and better nourished than any of the young men who ate the royal food" (Daniel 1:15).

**Keep 'right' and 'wrong' straight.** Many aspects of Babylonian cul-

---

[46] University of Florida, https://training.hr.ufl.edu > resources > job_aids

ture were not ethical or moral problems. Education, political structure and names are a few examples of customs that didn't offend him. Daniel could easily adapt to them without compromising his beliefs—no problem, no complaint!

But when it came to eating the King's food, Daniel had to draw the line. Doing so would violate God's law. It would require compromise and Daniel refused to do that.

Yet Daniel didn't throw a tantrum or verbally harangue the culture around him. Apparently, he never pouted about his lot in life. He didn't stage a noisy protest. He found a way to stay pure without alienating the ethos of Babylonian society. In fact, his godly actions influenced other people, too. This is the Daniel Model in a nutshell.

**Daniel led a life of quiet integrity.** His life displayed what you might think of as **"the 3 P's."** He modeled his life after godly values of *purity*, *piety* (goodness, godliness, holiness), and a *passion* for God. He led by example. He exemplified integrity, the core values of which are moral and ethical principles, soundness of moral character and honesty.

People from many walks of life loved Daniel. Even King Darius loved him and was distressed by the foolish law he himself had signed (Daniel chapter 6). He tried everything he could imagine to get Daniel out of the lion's den, but to no avail.

People loved Daniel, in part, because of his integrity. They respected his purity, piety and passion for the things of God. He proved that if we take a stand against the evils of our culture, we can do so without screaming, hollering or throwing things. People will notice our "3 P's." We can be part of redeeming the culture, not just rejecting it.

Condemning a fallen culture will often repel people, not redeem them, as God intends. If our behavior is critical and judgmental, God will not be glorified in that.

> **The Daniel Model includes engaging the prevailing culture with positive influence, while avoiding both cursing and moral–ethical compromise.**

A quiet explanation of why we won't participate in our culture's ungodliness, while treating others with respect, is more likely to get their positive attention and win an opportunity to explain our hope; "But in your hearts revere Christ as Lord. Always be prepared to give an answer to everyone who asks you to give the reason for the hope that you have. But do this with gentleness and respect" (1 Peter 3:15).

**Daniel's reward was a long life of faithful service and godly influence, even in an ungodly culture.** Daniel served both his Babylonian masters and their conquerors for an amazing sixty years. What a legacy of faithfulness and service in God's name!

Without purity, piety and passion for God, Daniel would not be known to our generation. He would've faded into oblivion and left no lasting influence on future generations.

**Learn a lesson in influence.** The Divi Divi tree is found on the South Caribbean island of Aruba. Because the winds blow almost constantly from the northeast, all the branches grow on the southwest side of the trees. You can always look at that tree and figure out the general direction. The wind doesn't accomplish the shaping of the tree in a day or a week. The force that shapes the branches is persistent in its quiet, yet determined effect.

Our influence forms and shapes others, too, even if we cannot see the change being slowly and tenaciously applied. We don't influence culture in a moment—it takes time, patience and godly determination. Don't hate the culture, as Jonah did. Nor should you let the culture shape you (Romans 12:1–2), as it compromised Esther. Utilize the Daniel Model and open a cultural crack where God's values can seep through.

---

### MOMENT OF TRUTH

God calls us to influence our culture positively. Tantrums and compromise are both unacceptable. Stand for godly values, and do it lovingly.

---

**INTERACT:** I grade my "3 P's," purity, piety and passion for God:

| D– | D | D+ | C– | C | C+ | B– | B | B+ | A– | A |
|----|---|----|----|---|----|----|---|----|----|---|

Sad state        Mixed reviews        My first priority

- I could influence _____ (name please) if I improved my:

_____

_____

_____

_____

- I plan to increase my ☐ Purity ☐ Piety ☐ Passion for People, by doing this:

_____

_____

_____

_____

- Up to now, my life has demonstrated ☐ Jonah's Way ☐ Esther's Way ☐ Daniel's Way. I want to change my approach by:

_____

_____

_____

_____

# 20

# WOMEN OF COURAGE

**JOURNEY TO LEADERSHIP AND VISION**
— Deborah and Jael —
(Judges 4–5)

## GOD USES WHOM HE CHOOSES

Deborah was chosen by God to be Israel's judge during an existential crisis in the land. It was very unusual for a woman to lead Israel. Jezebel and Athaliah were ruling queens, but never sanctioned by God. The only approved female who appears in the Old Testament ruling class is Deborah. A few other women were de facto leaders in listings and other accounts, but none held an official position as Deborah had. She was also a **Prophetess, speaking to God for the people and speaking for God to the people.**

Judges were considered elders in the pre-kingdom centuries between Joshua's generation and King Saul. As qualifications for shepherds of God's chosen people, the Old Testament lists "elders, leaders, judges and officials" more than once. If you notice the decidedly male nature of Israel's leadership, you're not mistaken. But God trusted this remarkable woman, Deborah, to lead His people and Jael to carry out His instructions during this unsettled time in their history.

Deborah was a woman of proven wisdom, courage and leadership. She was called "a mother in Israel." She was so highly regarded that she had her own tree, "the Palm of Deborah" (Judges 4:5), under which she held court as a judge. She wielded authority from God Himself to guide a nation that knew little about God and seemed indifferent to Him. "In those days Israel had no king; everyone did as they saw fit" (Judges 21:25). This was the society in which Deborah led Israel for God.

**Barak was a key figure in God's plan for Israel's liberation.** Deborah told Barak, "The Lord of Israel commands you to take ten thousand soldiers and lead them to Mount Tabor. There you will find Sisera, the commander of Canaan's army. God will deliver him into your hand for destruction."

> Everything rises and falls on leadership... leadership is influence.
> – Dr. John Maxwell

Barak was a trusted military leader, respected by the people. Apparently, he had enjoyed success in the past and the ragtag army of Israel would follow him into battle.

Not so fast! Apparently **Barak came up short on the bravery scale.** He responded to Deborah's instructions, "If you go with me, I will go. But if you don't accompany me into battle, then I will not budge."

"Of course I'll make the journey with you," she responded. "But because of this, you won't get the honor of liberating Israel from the Canaanites. Instead, God will bring down General Sisera at the hands of a woman."

When Deborah and Barak arrived at the battlefield, she told him, "Go! This is the day the Lord has given Sisera into your hands. God has gone ahead of you to make all the arrangements." As God fought for Israel, the Canaanite army was utterly destroyed.

**Jael was the woman with the plan.** This remarkable woman knew what had to be done, and her courage outshined Barak's timidity. When the Israelite army routed Sisera, he fled to a house where he thought he would be safe. Maybe he knew Jael's husband, Heber, of Israel's Kenite clan.

Jael went out to meet Sisera and invited him inside, where he could rest and hide until the coast was clear.

"I'm thirsty," he told her. "Please get me some water." Jael did him one better—she brought milk and covered him with a blanket. "If anyone comes by looking for me, tell them I'm not here," he instructed her.

But Jael's plan had a different ending. Anyone—man or woman—could have been repulsed by the bloody task. But Jael showed her grit. She took a long tent peg and drove it through his temple into the ground as he lay sleeping. She put actions to her determination and struck a blow for God's chosen people.

## THE VICTORY WAS A TEAM EFFORT

**God used Deborah, Barak, the Israelite army, and ultimately, Jael to liberate His people.** Victory is seldom a one-man or one-woman affair. True, each individual Christian needs God's help to be victorious over the enemy of their soul. Personal victory is a prerequisite for successful spiritual living in today's challenging world. Other Christians can and should support their sisters' and brothers' pursuits of faith. Everywhere we go, God plans for us to be functioning members of His team. We can be blessed by our Christian teammates. But we also need to bless them in tangible ways modeled by Christ Himself.

The list would be extensive of stars who the rich New York Yankees have bought to help them win World Series championships. Sometimes this famous-names-above-teamwork strategy worked. Sometimes it failed spectacularly. Often it was the lesser-known supporting cast of players who made huge contributions to the Yankees' baseball championships.

Famous Hall of Fame football players like Tom Brady, Emmitt Smith and Jerry Rice have won Super Bowls. But never without the dedicated teamwork of their blockers, defensive players and special teams' grunts. Unsung teammates often play quiet but vital roles behind the scenes. Even though these non-stars can easily be overlooked, the success their teams enjoy would be impossible without their unselfish contributions.

The same is true in non-sports arenas of human experience. The surgeon who saves dying patients, the CEO who leads the corporation to amazing profits, and the famous pastor of the megachurch; all are the face of their organizations. But none would be where they are without the behind-the-scenes nurses, the faceless assembly line workers, the deacons and Sunday School teachers and custodians (and pie bakers) who make their own modest but important contributions to the teams of which they are a part.

**Deborah, Barak and Jael teamed up to deliver Israel from the Canaanites.** National liberation and personal liberty are surely more important than World Series and Superbowl victories. This team's task was both daunting and crucial. Israel, though stubborn and often fickle, needed God's deliverance.

Teamwork provides the impetus from which you can **"expect great things"** *from* **God and "attempt great things"** *for* **God.**[47] Israel's victory over the Canaanites may have featured a few players prominently, but *the entire team was indispensable. And vital within a team is its leadership.* It offers a huge advantage in the success of any endeavor.

Leadership guru Dr. John Maxwell says, **"A leader knows the way, goes the way and shows the way. The power of leadership is the power to influence and motivate people to change, grow and achieve common goals."**[48] Deborah's and Jael's journey is historical proof of that universal truth. A team of more than ten thousand succeeded as it fol-

---

[47] From a sermon by missionary to China, William Carey in 1792, quoted in www.tabletalkmagazine.com
[48] The Power of Leadership – JMTcom: Maxwell Leadership Certified Team (johnmaxwellteam.com)

lowed the leaders God recruited, gifted, empowered and sent forth to achieve His purposes.

**Do you see what I see?** Leaders provide **the vision** for the great things Christians attempt in the name of the Lord. "Vision describes where we are headed: A picture of the future that produces passion. It is a **clear picture of God's preferred future…Vision is where you are going** and how the mission of God looks in your context"[49] (emphasis added).

Deborah's leadership provided vision for the team. Catching her vision, people like Barak and Jael and the rank–and–file soldiers stepped forward to make "God's preferred future" a present reality. Someone has said, **"If you aim at nothing, you're sure to hit it."** Without God–given vision, it doesn't matter how good your aim is, you will miss.

## GOD FULFILLED HIS PERFECT PLAN THROUGH IMPERFECT PEOPLE

God loves **accomplishing the extraordinary through ordinary people** whom He empowers for the common good. There's a tendency in American society to make our heroes into idols. It's not advisable, but we do it anyway.

In 2009, a US Airways pilot named Chesley "Sully" Sullenberger and his **flight team saved an entire planeload of passengers** when the plane struck a flock of birds in midair and lost both engines. Sully and co–pilot Jeffrey Skiles were able to land the aircraft in the Hudson River, just off midtown Manhattan. There were no serious injuries from what could have been a huge disaster. The incident became known as "The Miracle on the Hudson," and the crew was hailed for their quick thinking and performance under pressure. In fact, the entire team was awarded the Master's Medal of the Guild of Air Pilots and Air Navigators in recognition of their "heroic and unique aviation achievement."

---

[49] www.lifeword.org

When asked about his heroism, Sully shrugged it off and said that he had simply done as he was trained to do. It never occurred to him, at the time, that he might be hailed as a hero. I'm reasonably sure that none of the crewmembers were perfect people, as we might pretend our heroes are.

**Deborah was "a mother in Israel."** This remarkable woman had many admirable qualities. We know she was special in her time and place. God chose her, ordinary as she may have been, to deliver His people. In her own words, Deborah was affectionately thought of as Israel's matron. But we may be sure that she had her imperfections. None are righteous on their own. Isaiah wrote that all our (self–) righteousness is nothing more than filthy, bloody rags.

**Barak will be forever known as capable and chosen by God.** But he'll also be thought weak for his refusal to lead the war effort without Deborah's patronage. Together they marched the small army, probably carrying farming tools, into battle against far supe-

---

**BTW**

- **General Barak.** Character flaws are army issue for military men of high rank.

- Patton physically abused a soldier with PTSD; Grant was a failure at almost everything except making war; Montgomery refused to go into battle until every little detail was to his liking.

- Barak was a good military man but refused to fight without Deborah's coattails.

- He led a victorious army but the credit went to two remarkable women.

- **THE LESSON:** *God can do great things through the quirkiest people. He can even use ungodly people to achieve His goals (Pharaoh, Cyrus, Nebuchadnezzar).*

- *In fact, God even uses non-humans, like hornets, for example, because His planetary will IS going to happen, no matter what. He is sovereign (all–powerful).*

rior forces equipped with real weapons. God accomplished an extraordinary military victory with an ordinary 'chicken' at the front.

**Jael did the dirty work.** Scripture says very little about the woman who actually got her hands bloody in the messy business of warfare. Since God decided to use her, we can at least surmise that she was more-or-less ordinary in most ways. **She was not perfect. But she was available and obedient,** the sure mark of a successful person in God's economy. The resulting victory liberated the Israelites from bondage. The journey of Deborah, Barak and Jael brought about peace. Their leadership freed Israel from bondage for forty years. They enjoyed self-rule, out from under foreign oppression, for a full generation as they turned once again to God, their King.

After Deborah's inspired leadership was in the rear-view mirror, the Israelites sadly resumed their chaotic cycle of faith, complacency, disobedience to God, political, social and military conflict, and another plea to God to rescue them from their enemies. The dearth of leadership and vision was a curse from which Israel struggled for centuries.

## THE SONG OF DEBORAH

Things were so bad in Israel, before Deborah's, Barak's and Jael's war that "the highways were abandoned; travelers took to winding paths" (Judges 5:6) just to avoid the brutal Canaanites. To make things worse, all the weapons of war in Israel had been confiscated by their oppressors.

Fear stalked the land like COVID-19. Finally, Israel cried out to the God they had previously abandoned. He began to raise up leaders with the vision to deliver Israel. Liberation became a possibility, then a reality.

After the conflict against Canaan was won, Deborah and Barak sang a duet intended not only to celebrate their victory, but also to enter it into the oral tradition of recorded history for future generations. **Some in Israel saw what could be, and asked, "Why not?" Others saw**

**only the way things were and ran for cover.** President John F. Kennedy said, *"There are those that look at things the way they are, and ask 'Why?' I dream of things that never were—and I say: 'Why not?'"*[50]

There are many off-kilter answers to this idealistic question. Most sprout from the basic sin nature of humankind. Thanks to our father, Adam, we're greedy, selfish, proud and deceitful. Those sinful qualities often keep us from envisioning the best; we're even less likely to achieve it. They explain clearly why 'the best' so seldom becomes a reality.

A few intrepid souls in ancient Israel saw the oppression by the Canaanites and asked each other, "Why not seek God's deliverance from our enslavement?" After liberation by the hand of God, a *melody* of praise and celebration erupted from Deborah's heart, with Barak again singing *harmony* (Judges chapter 5). First, she identified those who embraced God's deliverance: Israel's princes, that "remnant of the nobles" (5:13), and "the people of the LORD." Then she added Israelite tribes Ephraim, Benjamin and Zebulun, highlighting captains from the clan of Makir (verses 13–15). Included among those who **saw things as God revealed them and asked, "Why not?"** were the "princes of Issachar" and Naphtali (verse 18). She even mentions the stars, which fought for Israel "from their courses" (verse 20). Nothing should surprise us when God is involved.

In contrast, Deborah pointed out, "In the districts of Reuben there was much searching of heart." The Reubenites "stayed among the sheep pens" (verse 16). Gilead stayed east of the Jordan River and Dan "lingered by the ships" instead of joining the battle. "Asher remained on the western coast" out of harm's way. Among those who sat out the battle were Meroz, "they did not come to help the Lord…" (verse 23).

Finally, Deborah praised the courage and decisive actions of Jael (verses 24–27). Her part may have been the hardest, as blood and guts

---

[50] Kennedy addressed the Irish Parliament at Leinster House in Dublin on June 28, 1963. He borrowed George Bernard Shaw's famous words of inspiration.

were directly involved. But apparently her hand never faltered, as she saw beyond the distasteful task to what God was birthing in Israel. Could I have done it? Not sure. But Jael did, and a mighty triumph resulted.

Deborah's song ends with the cryptic note, **"Then the land had peace forty years."** The dictionary explains *peace* as *a state of tranquility or quiet; security or order within a community; freedom from disquieting thoughts or emotions; harmony in personal relations...*[51]

Deborah's and Barak's journey to Mt. Tabor was a daring and obedient thrust, following God's leading to win the war, and with it, to win the peace. Who knows where your next journey might lead. Well, God knows, and He's eminently trustworthy!

---

### MOMENT OF TRUTH
Leadership with vision from God can accomplish immeasurable good in the world. He gives courage and wisdom to bring about peace.

---

MY PERSONAL JOURNEY: God has taught me this from my various leadership experiences:

_____
_____
_____
_____
_____

- Here's a time when I saw godly vision produce great things:

_____
_____
_____

---

[51] © Mirriam Webster, Inc., 2023

- This graph describes my leadership and vision:

  0   1   2   3   4   5   6   7   8   9   10

  I'm no　　　　　　　Sometimes　　　　　　I'm first–
  leader　　　　　　　I lead well　　　　　　class

- Here's how the idea, "God does extraordinary things through ordinary people" makes me feel:

  _____
  _____
  _____
  _____

- "In those days Israel had no king; everyone did as they saw fit" (Judges 21:25). How might this apply to the twenty–first century?

  _____
  _____
  _____
  _____

- Courage (and cowardice) show up in unexpected places. I ask God for the courage to:

  _____

# 21

# ROAD TO REJECTION

**JOURNEY TO VINDICATION**
— Jesus —
(Matthew 21:1–11; 27:22–26)

It started on Friday in an Atlanta courtroom. Brian Nichols grabbed a deputy's gun and killed a judge and court reporter. Then, he escaped through a window and fled. When it was all over, he had killed four people. The largest manhunt in Georgia history failed to corner him. Early Saturday morning he stuck the gun in Ashley Smith's ribs and took her hostage.

For the next seven hours, she calmly talked to him, fixed him breakfast, and convinced him that God had a purpose for his life. She told him reading Rick Warren's book, *The Purpose Driven Life*, had changed her forever. Nichols let her go, and she called the authorities. He thought about Ashley's words and decided to turn himself in.[52]

When the Jerusalem crowd cheered for Jesus to overthrow the hated Romans, He could've forgotten why He was here. The week before the Jewish holiday of Passover, the people celebrated Jesus on the way into Jerusalem. He was their hero. Soon, however, they discerned that

---

[52] Former hostage Ashley Smith recounts terrifying night that changed her life (to-day.com) • www.today.com/news/former-hostage-ashley-smith-recounts-terrifying-night

His purpose was to consummate a *spiritual* uprising that would reveal God's peaceful Messiah as King of kings.

Four days later, when Jesus sent the disciples to prepare the Passover meal, He quoted the prophet in Zechariah 9:9. The coming Messiah would be gentle, riding a donkey's colt, signifying His peaceful intent. Historically, kings armed for battle rode fierce warhorses. Kings coming in peace rode donkeys.

When the Jewish people realized Jesus had a different purpose than theirs, they turned against Him. When the Roman Governor asked the people what he should do with this innocent man, Jesus, they screamed over and over, "Crucify Him!" Pilate resisted their pressure. "What crime has He committed?" They ranted, "Crucify Him!"

When it looked like a riot would break out, Pilate said, "I am innocent of His blood." To which they gave their chilling answer that echoes down the centuries: "His blood is on us and on our children!" (Matthew 27:25).[53]

## THE PEOPLE'S PALM SUNDAY PURPOSE

**Politics and military conquest were the people's priorities:** The Roman Empire held Israel in its iron fist. Every Jewish person longed for a political and military leader who would defeat Rome. Much like today, Jesus's accusers thought the real power was political or military. "Might makes right!" declares, "Whoever is strongest gets to decide what's right

---

[53] Some may see this reference as inflammatory, but I hope not. Many bigoted anti-semites have hated Jews for the idea that they killed Jesus. But in the Father's divine plan, Jesus Christ, God the Son, had to die. That's God's plan. We could blame individuals who perpetrated the crime, and not all were Jewish (though none, besides Pilate, the Roman, Judas the fallen disciple and High Priest Caiaphas are named in Scripture). But Jesus's death paid the debt for your sins and mine. His subsequent resurrection has made eternal life a gift of His grace. "Father, forgive them," He prayed from the cross. "They don't know what they are doing!" God loves the Jews as His chosen people. We can do nothing less than love them, pray for them, and show our support in many ways in their hours of travail. God's Chosen People are precious to Him—and, thus, to Christians as well.

and wrong. Spiritual things are okay, but what we really need is a hero to put political power back in our hands!"

Jewish expectations for Messiah did not include Him being the Son of God. To them, He was a powerful leader. As Jesus's popularity grew, so did their great expectations. They wanted to make war, not love. They chose revenge, not forgiveness. They preferred power to peace. They embraced any means to gain their end, which was military and political sovereignty. That was *their* idea of Palm Sunday's purpose.

## JESUS'S PALM SUNDAY PURPOSE

Politics and military victory were not Jesus's priorities. His purpose was a spiritual Kingdom. Though most everyone around Him wanted a Messiah who would defeat the Romans, Jesus had a greater purpose. He was driven by His Father's divine assignment, bringing eternal, spiritual peace to a troubled creation.

In John 10:10, Jesus explained Himself. "The thief comes only to steal and kill and destroy; I have come that they may have life, and have it to the full." This is the quintessential purpose statement of Jesus's life on Earth: "I came so that everyone can enjoy abundant life, especially Eternal Life with Me in heaven."

> **When we're rejected for our faith, it can end in redemption for others through Jesus Christ.**

**Jesus brought peace through love, not power through war.** Jesus knew that love conquers everything. But they weren't interested in love. He knew that love is eternal, but they were focused on temporal power. Love was secondary to them. When expectations did not align, disillusionment set in, and rejection soon followed. And yet, love wins in the end.

## JESUS AND THE PEOPLE WERE AT CROSS PURPOSES

Their shouts of support on Palm Sunday became shouts of rejection on Good Friday as they screamed for Him to die. The physical was preferred over the spiritual, temporal over timeless, visible over invisible. Power trumped peace. The people's disappointment in unmet expectations led them to turn against Him. Their purpose went unfulfilled; Christ's purpose, to save humanity, was set in motion, even though rejection came first.

**Jesus knew on Sunday what would happen on Friday.** He could've tried to stop Friday's rejection and death by giving in to the people's wishes. Instead, He embraced the rejection in order to redeem fallen sinners.

Do right, despite rejection, regardless of the consequences. How many people make bad short-term decisions and then discover those choices have long-term damaging effects? That's what happens when we decide to do wrong, maybe even for what seems like honorable reasons. Jesus showed us that staying

### BTW

- ΙΧΘΥΣ Have you wondered about the 'fish' symbol, and how persecuted Christians used it?

- IChThUS (Greek for 'fish'): First letters stood for "**Jesus Christ, God's Son, Savior.**"

- You could draw a fish as secret identification to others who knew its hidden meaning.

- When admitting you were a Jesus follower could cost you your life, the common shape was drawn on a surface to identify yourself as a believer.

- The local authorities were unlikely to see the Ichthus as an ID badge. So, connection could be made with fellow Christians with decreased risk.

- We can appreciate the 70–million faithful Christians who have given their lives for Christ, Who is our IChThUS.

true to our purpose-driven life is worth dying for. Do the right thing, no matter what the results. To God's most faithful followers, survival is not uppermost. Trust and obedience are. If our faith leads to rejection, Jesus has been there ahead of us and will help us through.

God has a universal purpose for every life: "To know God and enjoy Him forever." He longs for a relationship with you. God also has a personal purpose for every life. He invites you to spend the rest of your life finding and fulfilling His individual plan for you.

**Trusting Jesus Christ as Savior is the beginning of a purpose jam-packed life.** Every person is a sinner (Romans 3:23). God has decreed that even the smallest sin will receive the death penalty (Romans 6:23). But wait, there's Good News. Jesus Christ died on the cross in your place, to take your blame, so you don't have eternal punishment (Romans 5:8). Finally, God has a wonderful, discrete purpose for you that begins with faith in Him (Romans 10:9, 10, 13).

**Jesus paid the price for His purpose.** For Jesus, fulfilling His life's purpose meant rejection, humiliation, and, ultimately, death on the cross. His obedience to death (Philippians 2:5–11) resulted in reconciliation for the rest of us.

Only God knows what your life of purpose may cost. Honestly, it won't be all hearts and flowers, fun and games. But life *without* God's purpose is no bed of roses either. Picture a long, frustrating existence bound to a hostile person. That's a little taste of life without God's purpose.

Choose God's path for your purpose-motivated life. See what wonderful things He will do for you and, through you, for others.

**MOMENT OF TRUTH**

Palm Sunday's cheering crowds rejected Jesus on Good Friday. They didn't accept His purpose. Since He was faithful to God's plan for Him, we can be reconciled with Him and make our own purpose–driven journey through life.

Let this YouTube song touch your life: The Wonderful Cross [with lyrics] - Chris Tomlin & Matt Redman

# BEEN THERE, DONE THAT

## AN EPILOGUE

In mid-September 2021, our lives changed forever. Kathy was rushed to the Emergency Room in Grand Rapids, Michigan (2,000 miles from home), with respiratory failure. For ten days she fought for life without my help, struggling with what would eventually be called "long COVID." Twenty days in ICU and another twenty-two days in sub-acute rehab got her stable enough that we were able to make our way back to our home in Olympia, Washington. Today, at our new home in Florida, she's much better but still suffering the effects of her near-death experience and learning to function again. So, when it comes to life's critical journeys, we've "Been there, done that!"

While resting at our daughter's Michigan home before making the nine-day journey westward, Kathy suggested I write a book that could influence our eight grandchildren to become more like Jesus. When I discussed *BEING LIKE JESUS: 100 Days to More Success, Satisfaction and Living on Purpose* with publisher Michael Stickler of Leadership Books, Inc., he asked if I had any other books up my author's sleeve.

The short answer was *yes*. I had written three or four chapters and outlined more than a dozen more. It was a book about examining the life-changing journeys of famous Bible characters. **The takeaway is how those journeys apply to everyday life for people in the twenty-first century.** Over a year later, the end result is this book. Without Michael

Stickler's confidence in me, *JOURNEYS From Here to Eternity* might never have seen its first sunrise.

If this book has blessed its readers half as much as writing it has blessed Kathy and me, then my purpose is achieved. After a long life of youth and music ministry, lead pastoring, editing my denomination's magazine, teaching communication and comparative religions plus Bible and Theology subjects at several colleges/universities, and serving as interim Academic Dean at Covenant Bible Seminary in suburban Tacoma, Washington, I am enjoying the fruits of fulfilling service to Jesus Christ, a faithful and talented wife, three great daughters and their husbands and eight wonderful grandchildren.

Our daily prayer is that you will **find encouragement and direction for your journeys.** We want you to maximize the benefits of a future that God is navigating in your lives in unexpected directions.

Thank you for reading *JOURNEYS From Here to Eternity*. May you accomplish more for Jesus than you ever expected. May His wealth enrich your life and those you touch. May His grace become the theme song of your existence. And may His love transform you from who you were before you read this book to a gleaming, radiant child of God, a practitioner of ever more joyful living and effective service to Him and His people.

Dr. Curtis Alexander<br/>Palmetto, Florida, August, 2024

*Dr. Alexander spent forty years pastoring in Ohio, Michigan, Illinois and Washington states. His D.Min was earned at Bethel Seminary, St. Paul MN. He also ministered as an editor of his denominational magazine, a professor of comparative religions, interpersonal and speech communication and various Bible and theology subjects at undergraduate and seminary levels. He finished his ministry as Academic Dean at Covenant Bible Seminary in suburban Tacoma, WA.*

www.ingramcontent.com/pod-product-compliance
Lightning Source LLC
Chambersburg PA
CBHW070055080526
44586CB00013B/1071